NOW THAT'S
HOW YOU
LEAD
SDR TEAMS

EMANUEL "E.R." CARPENTER

TABLE OF CONTENTS

Part 3 — Rewarding SDRs

Part 4 — Career

INTRODUCTION

I lied.

Sort of...

I told everyone that I had written my last book. And I believed it at the time. Even though BookAuthority named it one of the top 69 sales prospecting books of all time, the success of *Brain Dump:167 Tips and Tricks from a Six-Figure Sales Prospecting Legend* led me down a different path.

Entrepreneurship.

A couple of years after *Brain Dump* was published, I started SDR Master Class. The e-commerce website used the power of video to deliver pre-recorded lectures, e-books, and even SDR-themed apparel. The goal of the courses was to help SDR candidates find their first jobs, to help working SDRs to exceed their quotas, and to help SDRs prepare for closing roles or leadership roles.

While many SDRs took advantage of the How to Go from SDR to SDR Manager video course from SDR Master Class, they reached out to me after getting the manager job to ask, "How do I do this job on a day-to-day basis?"

I wanted to help them. That's why I wrote this book.

It was a tough decision to write this book. I thought about creating another video course to address the challenges of leading SDR teams. However, there were just too many topics to cover to give this subject matter its proper due.

Not to mention that the success of *Brain Dump* and SDR Master Class helped me to secure bigger and better sales development leadership positions. With the new responsibilities, I felt like I would never have the time to write another book.

And to be perfectly honest, I didn't think there was a large enough market of SDR leaders and BDR leaders out there who would want to buy such a book.

Then I had a change of heart.

As I led SDR Managers on my team at my day job and voluntarily mentored SDR leaders on the side, I realized that I was already writing the book. Granted, I was writing it in my head, in snippets, in emails, in Slack channels, and in LinkedIn posts; I was still giving those leaders the information they needed to successfully lead their teams.

If you don't know my background, I spent 13 years as an SDR, prospecting on behalf of Microsoft, VMware, Freightliner, Amazon, SAP, and more.

I cold called Tim Cook at Apple, spoke with him, and booked a meeting.

By the time I wrote *Brain Dump*, there were over 100,000 working SDRs.

Now, there are thousands of sales development leaders ready to lead them. I'm confident this book will help.

To be a great sales development leader, you are going to have to wear many hats; 16 to be exact:

- Trainer
- Coach
- Drill Sergeant
- Psychologist
- Administrator
- Data Scientist
- Marketer
- Event Planner
- Motivator
- Diplomat
- Recruiter
- Doer
- Referee
- Disciplinarian
- Keeper
- Outsourcer

We'll go through what it takes to be a master at wearing all 16 hats.

And you thought being an individual contributor was difficult? You ain't seen nothing yet.

The good news is that leading a team can be financially rewarding. It can be good for your career and good for your soul.

If you're ready to get started on being the boss, head over to the next page…

Part 1

DA BOSS

Chapter 1

KEEPER

Even though I learned to lead early in life, I had no intention of officially leading SDR teams.

As a child, I organized the neighborhood kids by starting an electric football team league. This was before video consoles like PlayStation and Xbox existed.

As a teenager, I organized a garage band called The Generics. I sang (horribly) and played my mother's piano (awfully). But Ed, Alex, Dean, and I rocked out nonetheless.

I was also captain of my high school tennis team and a class officer.

In the military, I was a squad leader.

Later in life, I taught myself how to be a great SDR by reading Anthony Parinello books. They worked, and I became the best SDR in the company.

Years later, I was content with being the top SDR in the company and earning six figures. But I also enjoyed being a team leader. You know, that in-between-role that allows you to coach without dealing with the hiring, the firing, and the babysitting. I was still an SDR, just an SDR+.

Before becoming an SDR, I was an AE for an orthopedic shoe manufacturer. After that, I was an SDR at six different companies in 13 years. Then just before my 50th birthday, that sixth company laid me off along with the rest of the SDR team.

After the success of my book and earning my way to making six figures, I felt that being an SDR and helping other SDRs was calling.

So, I did something drastic.

After 10 years in the city, I uprooted my family from Atlanta to New York City to take yet another SDR job.

It was a disaster.

At this HRIS software firm, AEs refused to take meetings I set with interested prospects if they were under contract with a competitor. I thought it was silly to refuse meetings with people who were interested in how we could help them.

My family hated the freezing weather and the concrete jungle.

We couldn't find an affordable place to live so our temporary stay at a hotel became long term.

And I was the oldest SDR in this rap-music-blasting office full of twenty-somethings.

Then two things happened that helped me realize I needed to make a change.

First, one of the SDRs, "Jarod," approached me at a team outing after a few drinks and asked, "Dude, how old are you?" In other words, why are you a 50-year-old SDR? And it got me thinking that maybe being an SDR had run its course. Although, some of the best SDRs I know are in their 50s and 60s and still doing a fantastic job.

Secondly, a few of the SDRs on the team read my LinkedIn profile, bought my book, and then came to me for advice. I enjoyed coaching them. I taught them how to prepone meetings, and it blew them away.

> Preponing is when you contact a prospect you've already booked a meeting with. You reach out and give them a reason to have the meeting sooner. They watched me prepone three or four meetings. I told each prospect that I was tied in a contest at work. Whoever booked the most meetings for the month would win a trip to Hawaii. If they would move our meeting from next month to this month, I would win.

> Most of the prospects would move the meeting because they wanted to help me win the trip. Although there was no real trip involved, I was able to go above quota.

It was exciting to see my peers hit their goals and earn more money because of my advice. Preponing was just one of many things I taught them.

Three months later, my former boss, Dan, told me that a startup back in Atlanta was looking for someone to develop and lead their SDR team. This would start off as a player/ coach role and eventually become a full-time manager position. I went through four rounds of interviews and liked what I heard from Mark, the VP of Sales. The next thing you know, my family and I were packing up the car and headed back to Atlanta. We were fueled by warmer weather, career progression, ageism.

One of the traits I admired most about Mark was that I felt he genuinely cared about me and the people he led. He asked about me and my family. He gave me great career advice. He even offered to give me a ride home when my wife, Sheila, needed the car at her psychologist job.

To be a great leader, you need to genuinely care about the people you lead. If you're only in it for the money, go back to being an individual contributor. Or go start a company and be a solopreneur. Leading SDRs is about making them successful and caring about their success.

There are several ways to demonstrate you care about the members of your team. Learn and memorize their first and last names. Learn their family members' names and refer to them by name when asking about them. Learn their pets' names. Your reps can tell the difference when you ask, "How is your husband doing?" versus "How is Jeff doing?" And don't forget to ask about their hobbies and interests outside of work.

Try to uncover this information on your first one-on-ones with the reps on your team. It's okay to put this information in a spreadsheet or jot it down in a notebook. Right before your next one-on-ones, review your notes. If your team is small enough, you'll memorize this information. In fact, I can still tell you the names of my former direct reports' spouses and pets from previous companies I've worked for.

I've worked for managers who didn't personally care about their team. One apathetic leader, "Linda," was new to the company I worked for. It took four meetings with her before she asked me about my personal life. By the way, are you married? Do you have kids? A bit late there aren't you, Linda?

Another way to demonstrate that you care is to develop your listening skills. Active listening is a skillset that many leaders don't possess. To be honest, I struggle with it myself sometimes. That's why it's important to read books or take online classes on sites like Udemy, Coursera, or LinkedIn Learning on how to be a good listener.

It can be challenging to go from being a competitive, top-performing individual contributor receiving all the accolades to allowing your team members to get all the credit. Giving them the glory is another great way to show you care about them. That means shouting them out in team meetings, on emails, in the Slack channel, and in your one-on-ones.

You can demonstrate you care by asking SDRs about the career path they want to take and by helping them get there. Do this by recommending which books to read, what webinars to attend, and what courses to take. If the path they want to take is outside of your org but within your company, introduce them to the hiring managers and facilitate those meetings.

I did this for "Chip," an SDR on my team who thought he wanted to go into marketing. When the marketing leader asked him to write a few blog posts because writing is part of the job, Chip decided that marketing really wasn't for him. He stayed on my team instead.

You might find it hard to believe but you can even demonstrate you care by terminating a struggling rep. Yes, it stings a little in the beginning. For most people who know that a firing is imminent, it's a relief when it happens because they don't have to worry about it anymore. Firing them can help them find the company they were meant to work for or the career they were meant to have.

I've even helped a few reps I had to fire by introducing them to other hiring managers, and they ended up earning more money than what our company was paying them. That's how you can be a friend and a keeper.

What about being a friend to reps while they are still under your leadership? While I'm a fan of being "friendly" with your reps, I'm not a huge fan of being friends with them. Make friends outside of your org or with other leaders at your company. I know there are situations that make this a challenge.

When you've established friendships on your team and then you get promoted to being their boss, it's difficult to let the friendship go. However, you have to be mindful of the tendency to show favoritism or the perception of favoritism.

For example, you may have to choose which reps get the best territories, which reps you recommend for a promotion, or which reps get to travel to a trade show in Hawaii. If your friend gets those opportunities, earned or not, the other reps on your team will not be happy. If you can be a boss at work and a friend after hours, do so cautiously.

I've socialized with fellow reps after hours and then later hired them at other companies after becoming a leader. I've even been tempted to forewarn them about privileged information. I held my tongue when one of them was insubordinate. And I've felt horrible after putting one of them on a performance improvement plan (PIP) and then having to fire them. Because of this, I prefer to join teams where direct reports don't know me personally. And I only hire top-performing reps I've mostly had a professional relationship with.

Just because you are not friends with the folks you lead, it doesn't mean you can't participate in fun activities with the team as a whole or even take a rep out for a meal on their birthday or because they crushed quota. I've organized pizza parties, bowling parties, and happy hours with the teams I have led. However, you don't want to be hanging out with the same rep every weekend like you would with a friend outside of work.

One of the hardest but necessary ways to show you care is to fight for your reps. They may need specific software to do their jobs. Executive leadership might want to change their comp plans to a goal less attainable. AEs may decide a lead an SDR provided is not qualified and that the SDR doesn't deserve to earn commission for it.

Make no mistake, you might win fewer than half the battles. But when you share with your reps the effort you took on their behalf, they will follow you through a brick wall because they know you care.

You can't fake caring. Try it and your reps will see right through you. They won't trust you. They might reluctantly follow your orders until they find a way to leave the company. And in the end, they will indeed leave to go work for a boss that demonstrates caring in the interview process or has a reputation for caring.

Caring with action is hard.

I've fought the battles with my own bosses when they wanted to change SDRs' commission plans based on outcomes the SDRs have no control over, like Closed Won deals.

I've written the multi-page business case to buy the software they need only to be told we don't have the budget.

I've spoken with the AEs and the AEs' bosses to get a meeting qualified before payroll gets run so that my reps can get paid.

And you know what?

I've seen the reps put in the extra effort because they know I fight for them. I've had SDRs follow me from company to company because they value my leadership. I even had SDRs I've led refer me to sales leaders they knew were hiring after I was laid off due to Covid-19. That's because genuine caring breeds loyalty.

Let me be clear. I'm not talking about being a pushover and giving your reps everything they want. If you do that, you will be an ineffective leader. Just because reps want something doesn't mean it is good for them or good for the company. Saying no and providing some tough love is a less-apparent way to show you care.

And just because you care about your reps, it doesn't mean you have to stop caring about yourself. If your pay is like most sales development leaders 'pay, your compensation is tied to your team's performance. When your demonstrated care for the team results in your own metrics being hit, you'll see how the power of caring for them helps you attain money, promotions, and accolades.

After you've established that you can and will care about your team, it will be time to get them trained. Turn to the next page to get started.

Chapter 2

TRAINER

Chances are, if you're in sales, you probably didn't earn a degree in post-secondary education. Yet, a large part of being an SDR Manager is training your team.

It's important that we distinguish the difference between training and coaching. Training involves teaching someone a new skill. Coaching, on the other hand, reinforces the skill that has already been taught.

There are more layers to training than meets the eye. Just like your 10th grade Biology teacher, it starts with developing lesson plans. In the SDR world, that includes playbooks, email templates, and call scripts.

Training also includes teaching SDRs how to use your software stack such as your CRM, research and data enrichment software, sales enablement platforms, and more.

Let's not forget business acumen. How to speak with prospects like an equal, how to conduct yourself at a trade show, and how to schedule your day to be the most effective are all examples of business acumen skills that need to be taught.

The good news is you don't always have to go it alone. Depending on the size of your organization, there may be people in place to help you with training. Sales enablement professionals can help with crafting lesson plans for SDRs. Sales operations professionals can teach SDRs how to use the software. Demand Generation folks on the Marketing team can teach SDRs how to craft meaningful copy for emails and social media.

You can also lean on your team leaders or the more experienced SDRs for some training. They can either lead training sessions or share recorded calls with less-experienced reps.

Now that we've addressed the what of training, let's dive into the how. First, let's talk about your playbook.

PLAYBOOKS

A well-written playbook will save you a boatload of time on training and coaching. It can include:

- Call scripts
- Email templates
- Objection-handling instructions
- Top competitors' strengths and weaknesses
- How to structure your day
- How to create a sequence or cadence within your sales enablement platform

- Top-performing sequences or cadences
- How to use the CRM
- Screenshots of your product
- Screenshots of your CRM, sales enablement platform, and other pertinent software
- Links to important training videos
- Links to marketing materials
- Rules of engagement with other SDRs
- Service-level agreements with AEs
- Territories and maps
- Target markets to pursue
- Top verticals to pursue
- Daily activity metrics
- Lead qualification requirements
- Buyer Personas
- Inbound lead routing instructions
- Quotas
- Research techniques
- Best Practices
- Contingency Plans

Your playbook doesn't have to be a static document. It can be a living document shared in a Google document or shared on SharePoint. You can make yourself the sole editor of the document and alert your reps when there has been a change.

A good way to structure your playbook is to start with a table of contents. You also want to include a brief introduction on why a section is important. For example, in the inbound lead routing section, you might write:

This section was written to give you step-by-step instructions on how to route an inbound lead so that we help our customers in a timely manner, and they don't turn to our competitors.

If writing is not your forte, consider enlisting the help of your sales enablement team or your Demand Generation team to help write the playbook. You should also consider outsourcing the project to someone with more experience. Companies like Upwork and fiverr allow you to hire gig workers on demand without overspending.

While we won't give examples of every section of the playbook, there is one that is crucial to your team's success: Call Scripts.

CALL SCRIPTS

Call scripts should serve as a guide to SDRs. It teaches them how they will conduct themselves over the phone in pursuit of booking a meeting.

There are three important sections of every good call script:
- Talking to admins (AKA gatekeepers)
- Talking to key players and decision makers
- Overcoming Objections

TALKING TO GATEKEEPERS

Your gatekeeper script should address a few subjects: 1. Getting the call transferred quickly without playing 20 Questions, 2. Leveraging the gatekeeper for guidance, 3.

Asking for the extension before the call is transferred to the key player or to voicemail.

TALKING TO KEY PLAYERS AND DECISION MAKERS

This section of your call script should provide what to say when the prospect first answers the phone. It should include a high-level value proposition. You can also include personalization techniques, various scripts for different buyer personas, asking the right questions, qualifying questions, and how to ask for the meeting.

OVERCOMING OBJECTIONS

Use this section to cover how to overcome the most common objections. A list of the most common ones are:
- I'm headed to a meeting.
- Call me back later today.
- Just send me an email.
- We're all set.
- We have a vendor in place.
- We handle it internally.
- We don't have the budget.
- I'm the wrong person.

For some ideas on teaching your reps how to overcome these objections, check out my book, *Brain Dump: 167 Tips and Tricks from a Six-Figure Sales Prospecting Legend.*

When training SDRs on making calls, break out the training in sections. Focus solely on gatekeepers in one session.

Talking to key players and decision makers in another. And overcoming objections in its own session as well. Use the sessions as building blocks. Later, you can work with smaller groups and train on all three sections of the call script. Or simply cover the longer training in your one-on-one meetings.

I've made over 183,000 cold calls as an SDR. Some of them I scripted. Others were scripted by clients I worked for including Microsoft, VMware, and Amazon Web Services.

As an SDR leader, I've listened to thousands of real-life cold calls and role plays. It's not as easy as an outsider might think. In order to get really good at cold calling, it takes planning, scripting, and practice.

In over 17 years in business development, I've found that there are five basics to having a successful cold call. Here they are...

ONE – Asking permission for time – Let's face it; nobody likes receiving a cold call. When you cold call a prospect, there is a 1% chance they are expecting your call. Acknowledging this fact and asking for permission for time is one way you can prepare your prospect to listen for a pitch while being sensitive to their busy schedules. Without seeking permission for time, you may experience getting interrupted or even worse, silence after your prospect ends the call.

There are many ways you can ask for permission for time. Some of the ones I've heard are, "Do you have 27 seconds?"

"Can I steal a minute?" "I'm sure you were not expecting my call." My personal favorite is, "Do you have a few seconds?" I couple this with an intro, and it sounds like this, "Hey Karen. This is Emanuel at SDR Master Class. I'm glad I caught you. I know you're super busy. Do you have a few seconds?"

TWO - Personalization – The next portion of the live call script is personalization. Unfortunately, most reps skip this. It's important to take the time to research and acknowledge potential pain or a potential threat to the prospect's company. You could also leverage information regarding what the prospect is passionate about. Find this information on their LinkedIn page, in their LinkedIn activities, or through news articles by following the company on social media or creating Google alerts about the company. Without personalization, you sound like every other rep promising the world and asking to schedule a meeting.

Personalized pitches sound something like these, "The reason for my call is I noticed your post on LinkedIn regarding the need to hire five engineers." "The reason I'm calling is because I was reading your article *The Seven Biggest Threats to HR Teams*, and it prompted a quick question." "The reason for my call is I saw that ABC Company is acquiring XYZ Company."

THREE - Value Prop – The key to the value prop is to allow prospects to get interested, to hear themselves and their most likely pains, and to hear how you can help. If you've done a good job at personalizing, your value prop should flow smoothly into the next sentence. "We help CIOs hire engineers in half the time it normally takes." "We protect HR teams from potential lawsuits by using software to encrypt employee data." "We help relieve the burden of acquisitions and mergers."

FOUR - Social Proof – Providing social proof can be as simple as dropping the name of an existing client in the same vertical as your prospect or as intricate as telling a specific story of how you've helped a company they've probably heard of. It could even be as simple as providing a real-life example to paint a picture in your prospects' minds. "For example, you probably heard about the winter storms that caused power outages in Texas earlier this year. We were able to help The State of Texas leverage our AI-powered software to alert staff and residents and keep their people and property safe." Just remember, brevity is key on cold calls.

FIVE - The Ask – Since the majority of SDRs earn commission on completed meetings, the ask is the most important part of your call script. It's rare that prospects even bother to pick up the phone these days, so it is crucial to take advantage of when they do by asking for the meeting while you've got them.

There are a few rules to follow when asking for a meeting. Ask for the absolute minimum amount of time you need to show a demo or have a discovery call. Ask for the soonest time available. I'm a big fan of having SDRs ask to meet the next business day because prospects show up more often and they don't forget what you wanted to discuss. Asking for the soonest time also helps SDRs make quota earlier and exceed their meeting goals.

If you've gotten a referral from the prospect's colleague and your goal is to book a conference call, downplay it by making it sound like you were aiming for a face-to-face meeting. "Rather than scheduling a face-to-face meeting, I was thinking we might just start with a quick, 15-minute phone call." Give the prospect a choice of two time slots keeping in mind that they might select their own third option. "How does tomorrow at 3pm Eastern or 4:30pm Eastern work for you?"

BONUS - Qualifying Questions – I don't think it is a best practice to ask qualifying questions on a cold call. That information should be obtained through research before the call or on a scheduled discovery call. However, many SDRs are required to ask qualifying questions before handing off a prospect to an account executive.

If you must ask qualifying questions, follow these important rules. Don't tell the prospect you have to ask these questions. Why? You will sound like an idiot. You cold called your prospect, asked for time and got it, and now you wanna make sure they are good enough to pass along? Get the freak outta here! Instead, make asking the qualifying questions sound like it's about making the experience better for them. A good sentence to use before asking qualifying questions is, "To tailor this discussion to your particular needs, I just want to ask you a few questions."

Don't ask for permission to ask the questions. (Is it okay if I ask you a few questions?) Just start asking.

Keep qualifying questions to a minimum. Three to five is enough. Combine questions if you can. Ask the most important questions first. You don't want to run out of time and end up not being able to book the meeting for your AE.

Listen for audible cues of frustration and hurriedness. When it sounds like you're about to lose 'em, stop your questioning. Either get your remaining questions answered in a follow-up email or invitation or explain to your AE why you were not able to get those questions answered. (Or better yet just share the recording of the call.)

ONBOARDING

If you work for a smaller organization that does not have a trainer or a sales enablement professional in place, you may be tasked with structuring your reps' onboarding schedule. You may even need to lead some of the onboarding sessions. Onboarding can take anywhere from a day to a month and is often combined with training.

It is important to include the following in your onboarding schedule:
- Meeting with HR so that SDRs can learn about company policies and sign up for health benefits and other benefits
- Meeting with department heads of other teams so that SDRs can better understand the company

- Product training for SDRs to learn about what the company sells
- Persona training for SDRs to learn about the type of prospects who buy what the company sells
- Meeting with account executives to strategize and learn how SDRs can best partner with them
- Tech stack training so that SDRs can learn all about the software needed to perform their jobs

Even if you have the luxury of having a trainer or sales enablement professional who handles training, it is important to collaborate with them to influence how the SDRs on your team will be onboarded.

TRAINING STRUCTURE

It's important to incorporate individual training and group training.

Individual training allows for more one-on-one interaction, privacy, and the opportunity for reps to ask lots of questions.

Group training allows reps to not only learn from you but to learn from each other. The questions and answers portion of the training can help those who are too shy to speak up by learning from the others. You can even have breakout sessions to allow SDRs to demonstrate what they've learned. Training your team as a group can save time as well.

Training is not just about call scripts and email templates. You can also use the time to train reps on your product, the software needed to perform, buyer personas, leveraging social media, writing and using sequences, and more.

Try to limit your training sessions to 30 minutes or less. The longer the training, the less the retention. Besides, your SDRs have other things to do like hitting their daily KPIs, booking meetings, and creating pipeline.

CALL RECORDINGS

If your organization leverages a sales enablement platform like Outreach or Salesloft or a conversational intelligence platform like Gong, you can use recorded calls to help train and onboard your reps. Having them hear what good sounds like and what not-so good sounds like can accelerate their knowledge.

Listening to call recordings can be done in a team setting too. You or one of the top SDRs can break down the call to illustrate what went well and what needs to be improved.

GUEST SPEAKERS

Oftentimes, we work with people who have the same title and responsibilities as our ideal buyers. Yet not many SDR teams leverage those people to pick their brains.

A great way to train your team is to invite those internal buyer personas to your team meetings. Ask them to explain what they do and how their day is structured. Get them to open up about their challenges and what it would take to get their attention. Ask them to listen to an SDR's pitch and provide feedback. Be sure to thank them for their time, and reward them if you can.

While you've got them, ask employees who have the same title as your prospects to record a voicemail drop. It would be a peer-to-peer follow up encouraging the prospect to return the SDRs' calls.

Now that we have a solid idea on how to train the SDR team, let's move on to reinforcing that training through coaching.

Chapter 3

COACH

Coaching SDRs is arguably the most important part of the SDR Manager's job. However, SDR Managers don't always have time for it. Quite frankly, many SDR Managers simply don't know how to coach. Let's unpack those two reasons on why more SDR Managers don't coach.

To be an effective SDR Manager, it is a must that you coach the SDRs on your team. It reinforces the training they've already learned.

We've all been to the one-hour training lectures that are packed with information. We leave those lectures charged up and feeling good only to forget what we learned a week later. However, when a task is done repeatedly on a set schedule, it's easier to remember what to do. Combine that with holding ourselves accountable through quizzes and tests and coaching becomes even more impactful.

What about those SDR Managers who don't know how to coach? A lot of them were the top SDRs at their organization so they were promoted to leadership without going through any internal leadership training. So the only way they know how to coach is to teach SDRs what they did themselves to be successful. This style of coaching doesn't consider that everyone learns differently and has different strengths.

Some of the SDRs on your team might learn through reading. Others may learn through watching a video. And some might learn by watching someone else do it first and then mimicking. It is important to ask each member of your team their learning style so that you better understand how to coach them.

You'll also discover that different SDRs have different strengths. Some might be great at cold calling. Others may do well booking meetings through email. You've also got the ones who do better by sending personalized videos or by connecting on social media. While it is important to teach SDRs to have a multi-pronged approach to prospecting, it's also important to let them use their strengths to perform well.

Remember, coaching is not about giving SDRs the answers to the questions they ask. It's more about leading them down the path to solving it themselves.

For example, as a coach I let my colleagues know that I had a wealth of information on how to overcome objections via email. I conducted a class, provided reading materials, and printed out cheat sheets for them to use. But when the training was done, they simply forwarded objection emails to me and asked me how to respond.

At first, I let my ego kick in and gave them the exact words to type. But after a while, I realized that I was not helping them grow by just giving them the answer. So, I started asking them how *they* would reply based on the class I taught, reading materials that were provided, and printed information I handed out. Pretty soon, they stopped forwarding those emails to me. Instead, they started using their brains and figuring things out for themselves.

ROLE PLAY

An effective way to coach SDRs is to have them role play. Role playing allows SDRs to practice their skills in a safe environment. Although most SDR Managers limit their role plays to cold calls, others include how to run a discovery call.

Role play can be done in a group session or on a one-on-one basis. You'll find that some SDRs shine in a group environment, but others do better when the focus is only on them.

Role play can be a scheduled event, or it can be used in a pop quiz-like scenario. You could schedule a session with the entire team. You can use it to fill in the gap in your stand-up meetings. Or you could make it a part of your weekly one-on-one meetings with individual SDRs.

To make role play effective, it is important that you as a coach alternate playing the role of the prospect and the role of the SDR. When you play the role of the SDR, it allows the SDR to hear what good sounds like. When you play the role of the prospect, you can put SDRs in realistic situations based on your experience.

Let's be clear. The most likely outcome of an SDR making a cold call is getting voicemail. Be sure to include some voicemail role plays but don't make it the focus. Instead, you want to focus on the four parts of the call:
1. Conversations with admins (gatekeepers)
2. Conversations with key players and decision makers
3. Overcoming objections with key players and decision makers
4. Ask for the meeting

While no two call scripts are the same, the fundamentals typically are. Teach your SDRs the fundamentals on what to say in each situation such:

GATEKEEPERS:
- Use the gatekeeper's name if they say it when they answer.
- State your first name and company name then ask to speak with your prospect.
- Ask the gatekeeper a question to prevent playing a game of 20 Questions before getting transferred.
- Right before you are transferred to the key player, ask the gatekeeper for the extension.

KEY PLAYERS AND DECISION MAKERS

- Ask for a brief amount of time up front.
- State the reason for your call. Verbalize it. "The reason for my call is…"
- Tell the prospect how you think you can help them.
- Ask for the meeting on the closest day to today possible.
- Don't apologize for interrupting their day.
- Sound like an equal regardless of the prospect's title.
- Don't overtalk or interrupt the prospect.

OBJECTION-HANDLING

- Disarm the prospect with a phrase like, "That's not a problem," when you get an objection.
- Recognize the type of objection you hear to use the right objection-handling technique
- Ask for the meeting again after overcoming the objection.

Role plays can be time consuming. That's why it is important to sometimes delegate the duties to your team leaders or top performers.

When you feel that a member of your team has mastered talking to gatekeepers, talking to key players, and overcoming objections, take a break on it. Spend role play time with those who need it most.

One final note. Make role play as realistic as possible. Do it over the phone if possible. Do it facing away from each other if you are in the same room. Or turn off your cameras if you're doing it over Zoom. SDRs don't get to see that non-verbal communication from prospects on cold calls. They shouldn't see it in role plays either.

INSPECTION

SDRs struggle. It's important to know why. You can better understand why SDRs struggle through a thorough inspection process. It's important to get to the bottom of any issues or roadblocks your reps may be facing. Don't think of this as micromanaging. Think of it more like detective work.

A list of things you can inspect are:
- Titles and buyer personas SDRs are contacting
- Types of phone numbers SDRs are calling
- Types of account lists being built and contacted
- Sequence tasks SDRs are completing and skipping
- Number of prospects currently in a cadence
- Overdue tasks
- Most effective cadences
- How SDRs are handling objections over email
- If SDRs are asking the right qualifying questions
- Hitting daily activity goals
- Email open and clickthrough rates
- Voicemail messaging
- Process for sending calendar invites
- Handling no shows and reschedules
- Response times to inbound leads

In *Brain Dump*, I put together a self-inspection checklist for SDRs. It's a symptom checker for sales development reps to understand the root cause of an issue. I also list a solution to the problem in that book.

In this book, there is an inspection checklist for SDR Managers. Use it as a guide to not only identify the problems SDRs face but to also consider solutions to the problem.

I promise you that if you perfect your inspection process, you will be a top-tier leader. You'll know you are there when you can no longer be shocked about what information your boss has about your team's performance.

INSPECTION CHECKLIST	
Problem	**What to Examine**
Low on opportunities	Completed SDR calls
	Timely AE conversions
	SDRs qualifying
	SDRs pursuing low-hanging fruit
	Mix of verticals and target personas
	Behavior after booking a meeting
Low show rate	Show rate >85%
	True challenge or pain uncovered
	Meeting confirmation process
	Meeting reminders
	Time gap between booking and scheduled meeting
Convos not converting	Hitting daily metrics
	Conveying value to prospects
	Overcoming email objections
	Enthusiasm and confidence on calls

	Call objection handling
	Dealing with gatekeepers
	Multi-touch strategy
	Reaching high-level titles for referrals
	Dialing mobile numbers
	Amount of net new prospects targeted
	Open and click rates on email
	Conversation to meeting rates
	Sequences being used
	Asking gatekeepers for extensions
Low KPIs	Structured days, time blocks
	Time on non-KPI activities
	PTO days taken
	Distractions outside of work
	Accurate account and contact data
	Distractions like promotions or being passed over
Manager To-Dos	Sharing rewards and consequences
	Giving enough coaching time
	Improve inspection and finding deficiencies

Figure 3.1

COACHING FRAMEWORK

Over the years, through mentorship, classes, and webinars, I've pieced together an SDR coaching framework. It has been helpful in showing SDRs where their gaps are, working together in finding a solution, and holding SDRs and SDR Managers accountable in course correction.

First, it's important to establish a different agenda for coaching sessions than you would your typical one-on-one.

ONE-ON-ONES

In one-on-ones, most SDR Managers use an agenda similar to the one below:

- SDR shares wins and challenges both personal and professional
- Manager shares quota attainment and KPI attainment
- Manager shares trends and other pertinent information
- SDR shares the plan for hitting goal
- Manager discusses the path to promotion
- Remaining time spent on role plays or the session ends early

Use a platform like 15Five to document your one-on-ones. If you don't have a platform like that, use a Word doc or a Google doc to write your notes. Then share them with the SDR after every meeting.

While I encourage SDR Managers to continue having one-on-ones with the reps on their team, they also need to have coaching sessions. Coaching session agendas are much different than one-on-one agendas.

The entire session is spent on reinforcing training and demonstrating what was learned. The goal is for SDRs to continue to improve on a week-to-week basis.

In order to have a successful coaching session, you first need to identify a gap the SDR has. You can either do this through the inspection process shared in this book, or you can have the SDR self-identify a challenge they are struggling with.

After the coaching session, the SDR Manager needs to provide the SDR a written summary of what was covered in the training session. This doubles the chances of retention. It also holds SDRs accountable and provides a written document for HR should you ever need to put someone on a performance improvement plan or terminate them.

The magic of the coaching session happens in the subsequent session. Within the first five to ten minutes of the session, the SDR needs to demonstrate what they learned in the previous session. This is the best way to measure retention.

The coaching agenda should look like this:
- SDR demonstrates learning from previous session
- Questions & Answers
- SDR Manager coaches new subject matter
- Questions & Answers
- SDR Manager follows up with a written summary (This makes writing performance reviews a lot easier. And it helps with accountability.)

If the SDR cannot demonstrate what was learned, it's important that the SDR Manager cover it again in this session. You should not move on to the next subject until the SDR can demonstrate comprehension.

Demonstrated comprehension can be verbalized, written, demoed, or even displayed by completing a quiz.

SCHEDULING

How do you know when to coach and when to have a one-on-one? I like the idea of coaching SDRs in the 2nd and 3rd week of the month. They are busy getting amped in the first week of the month. In the last week of the month, they are focused on hitting quota.

A schedule could look like the table below:

Week 1	One-on-One
Week 2	Coaching
Week 3	Coaching
Week 4	One-on-One

Figure 3.2

Things come up, and schedules change as managers are pulled in all kinds of directions. So, it's important for SDR Managers to prioritize one-on-ones and coaching sessions based on individuals' performance and needs.

A-Players, the top performers on your team, may not require as much coaching as your new hires, B-Players, and C-Players (including those on a performance improvement plan). So, you should feel free to skip some of the A-Players' coaching sessions if you are pressed for time. In fact, most of them would prefer that you leave them alone to continue crushing it.

You need to prioritize coaching the other members of your team. This means sticking to the schedule and only rescheduling in cases of emergency. If these SDRs require additional coaching, you can get that time by substituting an A-Player's session.

There will be occasions when you will need to meet with an SDR more urgently. For example, an SDR might be dealing with a sick family member. Or an AE might complain because an SDR missed a vital inbound lead. Don't feel like you have to wait for the scheduled session to address a more urgent item to cover.

On the other hand, an SDR might feel that their need is more urgent than it is. In these situations, remind the SDR of your scheduled sessions and ask if the matter can be addressed then. Protecting your calendar is almost as important as coaching your team.

WEEKLY TRENDING

It's important to let SDRs know how they are trending towards quota while there is time to course correct. That's why I encourage SDR Managers to let SDRs know how they are trending every Friday. Forecast how they will perform by the end of the month based on how they are trending.

For example, let's say the quota is 12 qualified meetings per month. At the end of the first of four weeks, Cindy has two qualified meetings. Based on that trend, she will end the month with eight out of 12 qualified meetings or about 66% of quota.

Now you can use the inspection process if Cindy has fallen behind to better understand why she is trending below expectations. Then you can ask her what her plan is to hit quota because ultimately you want her to be accountable for her own outcomes.

COACHING INBOUND SDRS

The key to coaching Inbound SDRs is:

- Getting them to respond to hand-raiser leads (i.e. demo requests and free trial requests) in under 10 minutes
- Teaching them how to reach out to non-hand-raiser leads (i.e. e-book downloaders, blog registrants, and event registrants)
- Making sure they write professionally when responding to emails, online chats like Drift, and form submissions. You'd be surprised at how many SDRs can't write well. Some write professional messages with texting abbreviations. Get them to download Grammarly.
- Showing them how to find older, non-responsive hand-raiser leads and how to follow up with them (because fresh leads can dry up)
- Getting SDRs to treat inbound leads by contacts as inbound leads for the whole company, especially when the inbound contact is non-responsive
- Prepping them on how to become Outbound SDRs or AEs (because bots using Artificial Intelligence are slowly replacing Inbound SDRs)

CAREER COACHING

Nowadays, the SDR role has been designated as an apprenticeship. The Bridge Group's 2021 SDR Metrics Report says that the average tenure of an SDR is 1.8 years. In other words, after a year and nine months, they are ready to be out of that job.

Where they go from there varies from customer success, customer support, SDR management, marketing, and even the sales engineer role. A recent poll suggests that 71% of SDRs expect to be promoted to account executive (closing deals).

With that in mind, SDRs will expect you to help them determine the best career path and to coach them on how to get there. That means taking the time in your one-on-ones to explain their annual performance progression. It also means facilitating meetings with other department managers. You may even be tasked with creating a training program to help SDRs transition to their most likely next role, account executive.

Be sure to continuously check in with SDRs to see if their career objectives have shifted. Be a resource for them for getting where they want to go. Be a career coach.

Teach them to leverage books, webinars, and free online courses to better themselves.

When I worked at a call-tracking software firm, I was tasked with working with our sales trainer to develop a training program for SDRs who wanted to be promoted to AEs.

This firm considered the SDR role more of a bench for the AE role than a means for generating pipeline. SDRs could be promoted in as little as three months' time.

"Donna" and I leveraged our learning management system to create instructional videos, a discovery call library, product training, and quizzes to gauge progress. During my tenure, I watched eight SDRs happily get promoted to AE positions. This was a result of good career coaching.

When SDRs don't take to your coaching, you may need to take it up a notch. The next chapter explains how.

Chapter 4

DRILL SERGEANT

I'll never forget my drill sergeants at Lackland Air Force Base, Sergeant Host and Sergeant Miller. Basic training was scary and exciting all at the same time (but mostly scary). The reason it was scary was because of Host and Miller.

They yelled at us and made us repeat a task, like making our beds with hospital corners, until it was done perfectly.

They threatened to delay our Basic training progress by making us start back at Day 1.

Sometimes all they had to do was mean mug us to signal that we were in trouble.

Our days and nights were all structured for us.

Yet, it wasn't all bad.

After getting over the shock of it all, I started to realize that every action had a purpose. Sergeant Miller would embarrass the overweight Airmen on my team for putting cookies onto their meal tray. After Basic, the Airmen would leave 15 pounds lighter and much healthier.

Host made sure all of us drank two glasses of water before our meals. It helped us to get full faster. There was a rumor that they put saltpeter in the water to prevent certain "urges." Plus, marching in the hot San Antonio sun was dehydrating.

Miller would test us on knowing all the various ranks of the Air Force from Airman to General. Wrong answers would result in latrine-cleaning duties. After Basic, it was nice to just look at the insignia on a uniform and instantly know a person's rank. Super important to know when you are supposed to salute an officer. It's a big deal if you don't.

As an SDR Manager, you sometimes must act kind of like a drill sergeant. While most don't yell at the SDRs on their teams (You might yell at some call recordings though.), managers can create structure for them. They can also make sure SDRs stick to the structure.

POWER HOURS

An example of providing a structure for SDRs is giving them mandatory times of day to only make phone calls. Most people call them power hours.

Why give them specific times of day to make phone calls? If you know that having phone calls with prospects is what creates success, yet SDRs are not making phone calls due to laziness or call reluctance, you'll need to create power hours. Just like a drill sergeant, you'll need to ensure the tasks are being completed. You can either sit with the SDRs during this time, listen live through your sales enablement platform, or you can run a report after every power hour.

I'm not saying you should have SDRs drop and give you twenty push-ups for not making calls. You do, however, need to drill the importance of what making calls will mean to them (hitting quota, making money, and being able to buy what they need).

When I was an SDR Manager at a marketing software company, one SDR, "Storm," would notoriously start his power hour ten minutes late. I called him out on our Slack channel every time he was late: "It's Power Hour. Where ya at Storm?" After a few instances of this, he would storm out of the office mad because I had embarrassed him. My method was effective though. Eventually, he changed his behavior and started power hours five minutes early. And his improved performance earned him a promotion.

LIVE LISTENING

Some managers like to use live phone call listening and real-time feedback for in-the-moment training. It can be somewhat effective if the SDRs on your team are having lots of connects per day. Perhaps they use a power dialer to make over 100 calls per day.

I've found that live listening and real-time coaching isn't effective. It's disruptive and distracting to SDRs. It's also a waste of your time because the most likely result of a cold call is to get voicemail. Do you really want to be spending your day listening to SDRs leave voicemails?

Plus, I've found that it creates a bad connection, creates an echo sound, and makes having a normal conversation with prospects difficult for SDRs.

A better approach is to incorporate call recording. Then you can coach SDRs when they are not distracted. You can either identify calls on which to coach SDRs or you can ask SDRs to bring recordings of their calls they want coaching on to your meetings with them.

10 BEFORE NOON

Another behavior I instill in SDRs is to make some phone calls before noon. The earlier they can have conversations with prospects, the better chance they have of starting their day with a bang. From there, they can build on the momentum.

Making calls before noon also remedies laziness and call reluctance. First SDRs start by not making calls in the morning. The next thing you know, the whole day has gone by without them making a single call.

It's also a good idea to try to catch prospects before their day gets crazy busy. That's why my mantra is 10 dials by noon, preferably between 8:30am and 9:30am.

If I look at the data and see that an SDR hasn't made 10 dials by noon, I put on my oversize hat and let the drill sergeant in me take over.

STRUCTURED DAYS

A structured day doesn't have to be limited to power hours. In fact, I think they are important to incorporate for all the tasks an SDR has. That includes research, sending emails, social media outreach, internal meetings, and phone calls.

Here is an example of what a structured day might look like:

8:00 to 8:30	Coffee, morning meeting, check email
8:30 to 9:30	Power Hour
9:30 to 10:00	Send Follow-up Emails
10:00 to 10:15	Break
10:15 to Noon	Research New Accounts
Noon to 1:00	Lunch
1:00 to 2:00	Power Hour
2:00 to 4:00	SDR's Choice
4:00 to 5:00	Power Hour

Figure 4.1

Create a similar schedule for the SDRs on your team, especially the newer hires. (It should be a part of your playbook.) When they don't follow the structure, invite the drill sergeant in you to help them out.

END OF THE DAY REPORT

Most SDRs have a certain number of activities they need to accomplish per day. We call these KPIs (key performance indicators). Activity KPIs can be calls, emails, social media invites, texts, personal video sends, and direct mail sends.

It is important to hold SDRs accountable for their daily activity metrics. If you discover that they are not hitting their goals, you might want to have them report their activities at the end of every day. Sure, you could run a report from your CRM or sales enablement platform and do this yourself. However, having SDRs do this reminds them of what they are accountable for and psychologically prepares them for completing their activities.

Just imagine having 10 unproductive days in a row and reporting that fact to your boss every one of those days. It's a lot easier and less embarrassing to just do the work.

When you ask SDRs for their daily activity reports, they'll start to include why they were unproductive and boast when they are successful.

Some managers might feel like this is micromanaging. It's not. You are not looking over your reps' shoulders every 30 minutes and asking questions. You are simply holding them accountable for doing their jobs.

Your success is measured by how your team hits their qualified meetings goals and pipeline goals. If that means bringing out the drill sergeant in you then that's what you'll have to do. Repeat after me. "Drop and give me 20!" Twenty dials.

Not everyone is motivated by drill sergeant-like behavior. For those people, you'll have to use another approach. Head over to the next chapter to find out what that is.

Chapter 5

THE MOTIVATOR

Back in the '90s, a rapper named MC Hammer electrified concertgoers with his music, rap style, and some of the best dancing you'll ever witness. Known for his hit songs like, *You Can't Touch This, Let's Get It Started,* and *Too Legit to Quit*, MC Hammer became a multi-platinum, worldwide sensation.

Hammer had a reputation for including several musicians, deejays, and dancers as part of his concerts. However, there was one person in his entourage that always stood out to me.

His hype man.

He went by the name of 2 Big MC. And yes, he was big in stature. He was also big in keeping Hammer and the crowd hyped by yelling phrases like, 'Hit 'em where it hurts, Hammer!' 2 Big MC definitely motivated Hammer to keep up the energy while entertaining the crowd.

What if SDRs had a hype man (or hype woman)? You know, someone yelling, "You got this," right before a call blitz.

Or saying, "You crushed that call," after booking a meeting with a difficult prospect.

You should be that hype man. You should be that hype woman.

Any fan of SDRs who post on LinkedIn will tell you, being an SDR is the hardest job in the company. Typically, they have very little business experience, but they are expected to converse with the highest-ranking executives at a company. They spend most of their day getting rejected on cold calls and through email. The AEs they work with seem to never want to approve their qualified meetings so that they can get paid commission. To top it off, they have drill sergeant bosses all on their cases about daily KPIs.

You've been there. Remember what it was like to have a manager in your corner? Hyping you up? Telling you you're doing a great job? I'll bet it made you feel good. Made you want to come to work and crush it.

Remember having the opposite of that type of leader? They made it hard to get out of bed let alone go to work to make cold calls all day.

Your job as a leader is to motivate your team. In this case, we're talking about positive reinforcement. There are several ways you can do this:

EMPATHY

Chances are, whatever the SDR on your team is going through professionally, you've gone through too. One of the best ways to motivate an SDR during challenging times is to share how you went through a similar challenge. Most importantly, you will want to share how you got over it. I've found that the best way to do this is through a story.

"I hear you. I went through something similar when I was an SDR. Do you mind if I tell you the story?"

For example, I remember the time when an SDR fell asleep on the job. It was in the middle of a training session. To be honest, sitting through the training was like watching paint dry. When another manager noticed "Mickey" sleeping in the meeting, she sent me a message over Slack.

After the meeting, I pulled Mickey into one of the empty conference rooms. Before I warned him of why it didn't look good for him to be sleeping on the job, I told him my own story.

At a previous company, I had fallen asleep at my desk after a big lunch. Twenty minutes later, I awakened and began doing my SDR job again as if nothing happened. Considering I'm a heavy snorer, I figured someone had to notice.

A few days later, I got a call from my boss who worked in another city. He tells me that someone sent him a video of me sleeping at my desk.

I was floored. I thought, at least give me the common courtesy of waking me up to say, "Hey man. You fell asleep at your desk. You might want to go get a cup of coffee or something."

Imagine the impact that story had when I led with it before warning Mickey that he can't be falling asleep at his desk.

When I ended up at another company, Mickey followed me there because he knows the type of leader I am. One of the reasons he tagged along was because I am an empathetic leader.

PAINT THE BIGGER PICTURE

While SDRs are in the midst of a storm, it can feel like the world's biggest spotlight is shining on them. For the most part, the SDR job is just a job. It's not like SDRs are finding the cure for cancer or solving the world's hunger crisis. They are just getting strangers interested in products and services so that their companies can sell it to them.

While it may feel like the end of their world when they don't hit quota or hit their daily activity goals, remind them that it's only a job. Years from now when they look back at the moment, they will realize how insignificant it was compared to more important things in life.

On a different tangent, if an SDR feels like their job is not important, remind them of why it is. They provide valuable pipeline that leads to revenue! They also introduce many strangers to the products and services the company offers. And they educate prospects too.

PRE-GAME

Right before they attend a live trade show, get prepped for a call blitz, or study up before a discovery call, provide words of encouragement to them. Let them know of the confidence you have in them to get the job done. Ask them to mentally prepare by playing some "walk up" music that motivates them. Or even coach them to listen to a stand-up comedian online to calm their nerves.

A quick Slack, email, or text to convey your confidence in them will go a long way. I heard you've got a meeting with the VP of Marketing at Zoom today. I know you're going to crush it.

POST-GAME

After a meeting with the key prospect, take time with the SDR on your team to find out how they felt about the meeting. Offer to review "game tape" by reviewing the recorded call together and offering positive feedback. Tell everyone on your team about the awesome job the SDR did.

SLACK CHANNEL

If the SDRs on your team have their own Slack channel, be the force of positive motivation within it. Be encouraging.

Be motivating. Be funny. Help SDRs feel at ease and let them know you have their backs.

When they do something fantastic, don't just tell the rep they did a good job. Let everyone in the Slack channel know how good of a job the SDR did. As the old saying goes, praise publicly; discipline privately (more on discipline in the next chapter).

There's a reason people love motivational speakers. They make people feel good through the power of positive thought and reinforcement. You can do that too. It doesn't take a degree in psychology to be a motivator. Just treat the people you lead a little better than you would like to be treated.

I now dub thee the 2 Big MC of sales development. Now go and motivate your team!

There's another way you can motivate your team. This way is not as fun.

Turn to the next chapter to see what I mean.

Chapter 6

THE DISCIPLINARIAN

Well shoot. That was a complete 180. Here we were talking about motivating our reps through positive reinforcement. Now we're talking about disciplining them?

We sure are. One of the biggest mistakes SDR Managers make is that they treat every SDR the same. They are all rewarded the same way. They encourage them all to take the same career path. And they try to motivate them in the same way. But not every SDR is motivated by cold hard cash, a promotion to AE, and an attaboy on the Slack channel.

Some SDRs are motivated by consequences.

There are many ways you can remind an SDR of the consequences of their actions.

If you don't call your prospects, you might not make quota.

If you consistently miss quota, you will be put on a PIP.

If you don't beat the PIP, you can be fired.

If you get fired, how are you going to eat and pay your rent?

As a leader, it is your job to discipline SDRs when they don't do what they are supposed to do.

If you expect the SDRs you lead to research 10 accounts per day, and one SDR only researches three, you may need to discipline them.

If an SDR on your team is 15 minutes late every other day, you might need to discipline them.

If an SDR on your team missed quota six months in a row, you most definitely will need to discipline them.

It's an uncomfortable subject.

Being the disciplinarian is a necessary evil. It can be especially hard if you've been promoted from their ranks to their manager. But when you don't discipline reps who need it, things can get a lot worse.

The SDRs who follow the rules and do their jobs well will lose respect for you.

The SDRs who don't follow the rules and do their jobs poorly will treat you like a doormat.

The poor performers will get frustrated from not earning good commission checks.

Your team won't hit quota.

Worst of all, you will be fired if you are not driving your team to perform well.

When I was the SDR Manager at a software company in Atlanta, I had a strict policy that SDRs had to make at least 10 dials by noon. But when "Ramona" was promoted from Inbound SDR to Outbound SDR, I noticed that she made zero calls by noon. Zero. I chalked it up to call reluctance. I know it can be difficult to transition from contacting hand-raisers to cold calling strangers.

I gave Ramona a gentle nudge over Slack. Her behavior didn't change. Finally, I gave her a verbal warning in her next one-on-one. I simply told her that if she doesn't start making 10 calls by noon, we're going to be having a very different conversation in her next one-on-one.

It worked.

Ramona was making 15 to 20 calls before noon. She overcame her call reluctance, and she ended up earning a promotion to a closing role.

Discipline is not limited to the day-to-day activities of the job and making quota. You'll need to discipline the SDRs on your team for things like excessive tardiness, sexual harassment, getting drunk at a trade show, coming to work hungover, and more.

The best way to be prepared to discipline the SDRs on your team is to first provide them with HR's company handbook. They should receive this Day 1 and confirm that they have read it.

To properly discipline SDRs, you should create a process. For me, that process includes coaching, verbal warnings, written warnings and PIPs, demotion, and termination.

PERFORMANCE IMPROVEMENT PLANS (PIPS)

The first time I had to put an SDR on a PIP, I had insomnia for a week. "Jamal" was such a nice guy but the additional coaching I was providing to him was not affecting his outcomes. He was consistently performing under 70% of his goals, sometimes even lower than 50%. So, I had no choice but to put him on a PIP.

Most performance improvement plans are based on under-performance within a certain amount of time. Although the standard for the average PIP is three consecutive months below 70% of quota, I have seen some PIPs state that consecutive months under 50% was their policy. Many organizations simply take the average quota attained over the last quarter or over the last four to six months to determine if a PIP is necessary.

The following table shows the calculations for a sample PIP based on the average quota over three months.

May	50%
June	80%
July	70%
Average over 3 months	**66%**

Figure 6.1

If you've never written a PIP, start by utilizing your HR department. Chances are, they will have pre-written templates you can use to deliver the PIP to the poor performing SDR.

The PIP should have specific information, including:
- Reason for the PIP
- Verbal warning dates
- Start date and length of the PIP
- SDR's daily requirements during the PIP
- Conditions for being taken off a PIP
- Additional coaching dates and times
- Rules for taking PTO during this time period
- Consequences for not beating the PIP
- Signature lines for the SDR and SDR Manager

Back to Jamal. Unlike most SDRs on a PIP, he beat it. He worked his butt off to hit 100% of quota. After that, he became a top performer in the organization and never saw another PIP.

DEMOTION

A rarely used disciplinary action for SDRs is demotion. The SDR role is typically the most junior role within the sales (or marketing) organization. Obviously, you can't demote anyone lower than the lowest.

However, many organizations use micro-promotion strategies within the SDR team. This allows SDRs to reach certain promotions and raises based on tenure and performance. For example, an SDR 1 could get promoted to SDR 2 for exceeding quota in consecutive months. Or an Inbound SDR could be promoted to an Outbound role.

Step promotions also open up the possibilities to demote an underperforming SDR. Although it might be embarrassing and costly, a demotion is less drastic than a termination.

TERMINATION

And you thought I couldn't sleep when I put a rep on a PIP. Imagine all the melatonin I needed after the first time I had to fire an SDR. Not that they didn't deserve it. Multiple verbal warnings for insubordination coupled with failing to hit 50% of quota in three consecutive months sealed their fate.

If you need to terminate an SDR for the first time, here is what I want you to remember:
- Get HR involved during the PIP stage.
- Keep a "paper" trail of emails, Slack messages, and performance reviews
- Check in on your own mental health.
- You are probably helping them. Maybe you helped them discover what they are not good at so that they can land their dream job.

The disciplinarian role is difficult but necessary but I for one am tired of talking about it. Let's move on to something a little less depressing: administrative duties.

Chapter 7

THE ADMINISTRATOR

This chapter is dedicated to the SDR Managers who thought they'd be spending 90% of their time on coaching SDRs.

Nah, bruh.

At the most, you'll spend 30% of your time coaching SDRs. Instead, your days will be filled with reacting to immediate SDR needs (Those Slacks never stop!), approving PTO, meeting with other departments like Marketing, Sales Operations, and Sales Enablement, territory planning and re-assigning, and even writing comp plans.

That's why many individual contributors avoid becoming managers. You'll often hear them call management glorified babysitting. And while there is a small element of truth to the babysitting statement, a lot of the job is just administrative work.

This chapter will focus on how to deal with immediate requests, how to write compensation plans, and where to start with SDR territory planning and AE pairing.

COMPENSATION PLANS

There are three things you want to think about when creating comp plans:

1. Rewarding reps for a job well done
2. Driving behavior that leads to positive outcomes (completed meetings, opportunities created, pipeline creation, and closed won deals)
3. Protecting the company from overspending

Here are some options:

Outbound SDR Meetings Pay

Pay one flat rate for every completed meeting, for example, $100 for every completed meeting.

OR...

Use tiered comp for completed meetings to reward overachieving and discourage underachieving. It's a pain to calculate every month if you have a large team.

Here is an example comp structure based on a 10-meetings-per-month quota:

1-4 meetings - $50 per meeting

5-9 meetings - $80 per meeting

10 meetings - $100 per meeting

11 or more meetings - $150 per meeting

Opportunities Pay

If an AE creates an opportunity from a meeting and assigns a dollar value to it, you can use a tiered comp plan like the one above. Alternatively, you could create a separate bonus structure for the achievement. For example, SDRs could earn $250 for every meeting that becomes an opportunity.

You have to be careful here because now you are basing the SDR's comp on something they cannot control. I prefer using the meetings pay AND the opportunity bonus to drive behavior leading to good, qualified meetings set. Plus, some AEs who don't want to be held accountable for the pipeline will find ways to disqualify a valid qualified opportunity. You will need a solid Service Level Agreement between SDRs and AEs to determine what exactly is considered a qualified meeting.

Many organizations use some element of B.A.N.T.

Budget
Authority
Need
Timeline

I prefer a simpler criteria I call A.I. (authority and interest). If the prospect has a genuine interest in what you sell and has the authority to buy or influence the buying decision, SDRs should set up a meeting with an Account Executive as soon as possible. Remember, SDRs are the most junior salespeople within your organization. You'll want your more experienced reps getting involved as soon as possible.

There are some organizations that require SDRs to run discovery calls on their own. I think it works for your more experienced SDRs with over a year of experience. Running "discos" is much more difficult than setting up A.I. qualified meetings, and SDRs should be compensated more for them.

Closed Won Deals

To drive quality meetings, I encourage paying SDRs a percentage of the value of a closed deal if they initiated the meeting. This typically ranges from 1% to 5% of the first year's contract value. Again, since SDRs have little control over what deals close, you don't want their comp plans to be too heavily based on Closed Won deals.

If your organization is not comfortable splitting the commission on Closed Won deals between SDRs and AEs, you could simply agree to pay a set dollar amount bonus for them.

At one HRIS software firm I worked for, SDRs received a $50 bonus for every closed deal that they sourced. This was in addition to their qualified meetings bonus.

All Base, No Commission

I toyed with the concept of making the SDR job an all-base-pay position for a few years but could never get executive leadership and some SDRs to go for it. I wanted to pay SDRs the majority of their OTE in base plus a percentage of money for the closed deals they sourced. I thought this structure would reduce the number of bad meetings that SDRs set and would drive the quality of the meetings they set for

AEs. The problem with this structure is that it doesn't drive overachievement, so SDRs are not motivated to do more than the minimum.

Quotas

Quotas need to be achievable. If 70% or more of your team are not consistently hitting quota, it is probably too high. If too many people are achieving over 110% of quota every month, your quota is probably too low, which costs the company money. For example, if 12 out of 15 SDRs are hitting 150% of quota every month, you need to raise the quota before your Finance team does it for you.

Quota also needs to be based on historical data and company needs. Many startups creating the very first quotas for the SDR team simply use reverse math to determine quotas.

For example, let's say the Sales team need to close $10 million in revenue for the year. Based on historical data, we might see that the Sales team only closes 10% of their pipeline annually. That means they will need $100 million in pipeline per year.

Let's assume the pipeline goal is split evenly between SDRs and Marketing. SDRs would have a goal of $50 million in pipeline per year. Divided by 12 months, that comes out to $4,166,666 per month in pipeline.

If you know that the average SDR provides $500,000 in pipeline per month, that lets you know that you will need eight or nine SDRs to hit your pipeline goal.

And let's say the average deal size is $100,000. It would mean that SDRs will need to generate five qualified meetings per month to hit their $500,000 pipeline goal.

Just because SDRs have a pipeline goal, it doesn't mean that it has to be tied to their comp plan. If you can consistently see that five qualified leads equals $100k in pipeline, you could easily make their goal five qualified meetings per month.

Based on performance, marketing trends, and more you can adjust quotas based on what you've learned.

If there is no historical company data to rely upon, you'll have to use data from similar companies in the same industries. That's when it will make sense to join Slack channels like SDReady, LinkedIn groups like SDRLeader. com, and professional organizations like Pavilion and RevGenius. You can leverage those relationships to better understand industry standards.

Or if you come from a similar company, you can start by using the same quotas you used at your last job.

Inbound SDR Comp Plans

Since most Inbound SDRs only work inbound marketing leads, their quotas need to be based on the number of inbound leads received each month and the amount they can turn into meetings and opportunities. I typically use a tiered system and expect Inbound SDRs to convert a minimum of 23% of their hand-raiser leads (demo requests, free trials, etc.). Not all companies are the same. You should determine conversion rates based on historical data and industry standards.

I don't believe simple content downloads (e-books, whitepapers, etc.) should be counted because in my world over 95% of the leads don't convert. In fact, those leads are better suited to be given to Outbound SDRs. Since Inbound SDRs have no control of the volume of inbound leads received, I would not give them a set monthly quota based on a static number.

Let's say an Inbound SDR's OTE commission comp is $1200 a month. If the rep passes 23% of their leads, they earn the $1200 a month in my scenario. You can use a tiered system based on the percentage of leads converted to pay Inbound SDRs accordingly.

Here is an example comp structure I created for Inbound SDRs:

25% or more converted = 110% of OTE
23%-24% converted = 100% of OTE
19%-22% converted = 90% of OTE
18% or less converted = 50% of OTE

Accelerators and Decelerators

You'll notice that the comp plan for Inbound SDRs has an accelerator for overachieving and a decelerator for underachieving. You could use accelerators and decelerators in Outbound SDR comp plans as well. The goal is to reward overachievement and create consequences for underachievement.

You'll also notice that the accelerators are capped at 110%. It's intentional because I expect Inbound SDRs to be in seat for a short amount of time. They should be working hard towards becoming Outbound SDRs or AEs where the financial rewards are greater.

Allbound

If you have only one team that receives inbound leads and they source their own leads, they are an allbound team.

Consider using a point system for the various types of leads they provide to AEs and assign points to them to calculate commission.

For example, an inbound lead that's a hand-raiser like a demo request would earn the SDR one point because it's easy to convert to a meeting. An inbound lead that is only a prospect who downloaded content might be worth two points because it is a little harder to convert to a meeting. A meeting with a prospect at a company that is on an AE's targeted list could be worth three points because it's the most difficult to get.

From there, you can assign a dollar value for every point. For example, SDRs could earn $50 a point.

Ramp Quota

It's unrealistic to expect your new hire SDRs to hit quota within their first few months at the company. That's why it is important to implement a ramp quota that allows them to earn their full commission while they are learning.

This usually involves paying SDRs a draw they don't have to pay back. Most organizations do this for one to three months. Typically, they pay SDRs as if they've earned 100% of quota.

Some organizations pay the draw if SDRs achieve certain goals and milestones like hitting an abbreviated KPI goal or completing their cold call certification.

SPIFFs

I use electronic gift card programs like Rewards Genius and Kudos to financially reward SDRs for short-term achievements. I encourage you to use a tool like SurveyMonkey to poll the SDRs on your team. Ask them how they like to be rewarded for a job well done. Not everyone is cash motivated. Some SDRs like trips, booze, lottery tickets, food, time off, and more.

SPIFFs help to drive short-term behavior. You could use a SPIFF to drive SDRs to try a new process, to reward them for being top performer of the month, or to reward them for being the winner of a contest like a call blitz.

Base Pay

You can use national averages to determine base pay. The Bridge Group has an annual report that shows this data. In 2021, the average base pay for SDRs was $50,000 a year. The average commission was $26,000 a year. In cities where the cost of living is greater, expect to pay SDRs more. Given the higher level of difficulty for the Outbound SDR job (cold outreach) versus the nature of the Inbound SDR job (contacting warm leads and hand-raisers), Outbound SDRs typically earn more. Also, experienced SDRs will also expect to earn more.

Location-Based Cost-of-Living Adjustments

Some organizations pay SDRs more when they live in high-cost cities. SDRs command a larger comp in cities like New York, San Francisco, and Boston. While SDRs in cities like Mobile, Orlando, and Cleveland tend to earn less. The adjustment is based on the cost of living in each city.

I'm not a fan of location-based premiums. I think it penalizes SDRs of equal or greater talent who just happen to live in cities with a lower cost of living.

Now that many SDR teams are working remotely as the result of working during the Covid-19 pandemic, there's almost nothing stopping SDRs from saying they live in a high-cost area when they live in a low-cost area. (Some companies search the location of SDRs' company-issued computers.) Just imagine an SDR whose parents live in New York City, but they live in Tulsa. It would be a lot simpler to just treat SDR comp equally regardless of location.

As an SDR Manager at a new startup, you may be tapped to create, write, and implement a new comp plan. Even as a new hire to a company that already has a comp plan in place, you may be tasked to review and update the plan. You'll have many options to choose from.

Territory Planning

Territory planning is a lot easier when pairing SDRs with AEs who already have territories assigned. Most sales teams create territories based on one of three plans:

Geographically based territories

Simply assign territories to reps by splitting up the map. If AEs are spread throughout the world and are expected to meet face to face with prospects, they'll often be assigned geographic territories near where they work.

Size-based territories

These territories are divided by three sizes, small-to-medium businesses (SMB), mid-market, and enterprise (companies with the greatest revenue or most employees). Many Software-As-A-Service (SaaS) organizations divide their SDR teams by SMB, mid-market, and enterprise.

Vertically based territories

Other companies divide their reps' territory by vertical (based on what their prospects sell). For example, verticals could include automotive, hospitality, high-tech, real estate, and even government. Vertically based territories are extremely effective when the company has existing customers within the verticals. Prospects like it when your company has experience helping their type of company.

SDR/AE Assignments

As an SDR Manager, you'll have to determine which SDRs to pair with which AEs. You'll also need to determine the ratio of SDRs to AEs. While many leaders like the idea of assigning one SDR to one AE, oftentimes they won't have the headcount or the budget to do so.

A more likely scenario is to assign one SDR to two AEs or one SDR to three AEs. SDRs working on SMB accounts have a greater capacity to work with multiple AEs. Enterprise SDRs, on the other hand, can most likely only handle working with no more than three AEs.

There are advantages to assigning SDRs to more than one AE. SDRs get to "diversity their portfolio" and not solely rely on one AE to qualify opportunities and close deals. When one AE is out of the office, the SDR doesn't have to be limited on when they can schedule meetings. Also, if there is a personality clash with an SDR and an AE, they have other AEs they can get along with. Since SDRs are often mentored by AEs, having a good working relationship is important.

On the other hand, SDRs who work with one AE can be more focused in their approach. They don't have to worry about splitting their time and their outcomes among AEs. Plus, mentorship is even stronger when there is a one-on-one relationship.

Round Robin

Another strategy you can use is the round robin strategy. This is effective when AEs do not have assigned territories.

When an SDR books a meeting, it simply goes to the next AE on the list. You can even use a round robin approach when there are multiple AEs under the various size-based territories.

While it's cheaper to use pen and paper to remember which AE received a scheduled meeting from an SDR last, it is a lot easier to use a software platform like Chili Piper or Calendly to automate your round robin strategy.

Using a round robin strategy to assign meetings to AEs is the best way to ensure fairness and equal distribution of meetings.

Take Control of Your Calendar

As an SDR Manager, a lot of your day will be spent in reactive mode. If SDRs aren't unexpectedly walking into your office, they are sending you messages over Slack. Although some of the SDRs' needs will be time sensitive, not every request will be urgent. Let's keep it real. You've got other things to do than to react to non-urgent needs. Some of those things include:

- Approving PTO
- Meeting with other departments
- Meeting with your boss
- Presenting to executive leadership
- Interviewing candidates
- Writing business cases
- Sitting on demos for software you might need for your team
- Getting trained

- Planning contests and SPIFFs
- Calculating commission for payroll
- Eating lunch
- Taking time to think

To take control of your calendar, you'll need to set up the rules of engagement with the SDRs on your team. Instead of having an always open, open-door policy, establish one or two hours in the day as open office hours. Remind SDRs to leverage those hours for non-emergency needs. Ask SDRs if their situation is urgent or if it can wait until the end of the day or wait until their scheduled one-on-one.

Block off your calendar and put Slack on pause as needed so that you can focus on your most important tasks of the day.

There is another important reason to block off time in your day. This reason is a little more controversial. Turn to the next page to find out what that is.

Chapter 8

DOER

You are not going to want to hear this.

Just because you've become an SDR Manager, it doesn't mean you should stop outbounding.

I polled a group of SDR leaders on how they would react if they were required to keep outbounding in their leadership positions.

Here are the results:

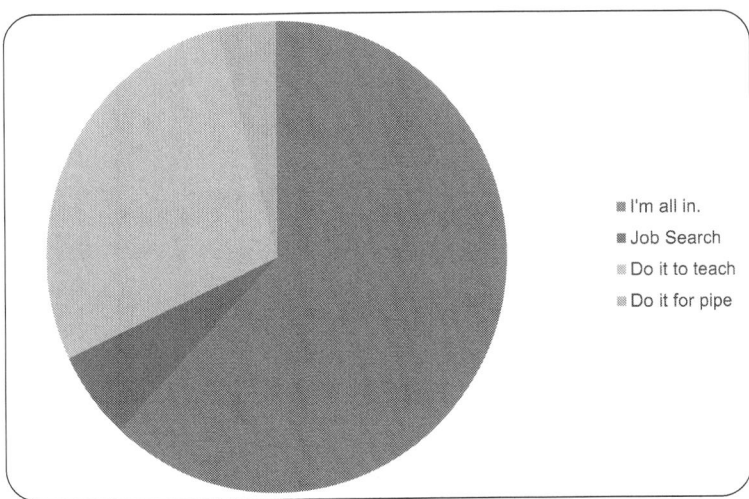

Figure 8.1

Yeah, I know it hurts, especially if you just got promoted out of the SDR role. But hear me out.

There are certain things SDR Managers do that distinguish them from being good leaders to being great leaders. Amongst those things are being nice, listening actively, showing empathy, being a coach, and treating reps better than you treat yourself. To really take it up a notch, it's important that you lead by example.

In my military days, we called this leading from the front. Picture an infantry battalion captain marching 200 troops into battle from the back of them inside of a tank. Now imagine that same captain marching those troops into battle from the front lines with his rifle drawn. In which version of this story are you going to be the most motivated? My guess is the latter version.

One of the best ways to lead by example is to run beat-the-boss contests.

BEAT THE BOSS CONTESTS

SDR leaders need to join their team in making cold prospecting calls. It's more fun when they make it a contest. You can run the contest one day a month or even one day a quarter. Whoever beats you in booking the most meetings wins a prize. Here are five reasons why the contest is important:

1. Walk a mile in their shoes. There is no better way to truly understand what SDRs go through every day than to do their job for a day. It doesn't matter if you

were an SDR two months ago, an SDR two years ago, or you've never been an SDR.

2. Earn their respect. Joining your team on calls lets them know that you're not above doing the job yourself. You gain even more respect when you book meetings and share your recordings of conversations you've had with prospects. Don't limit your sharing to just meetings booked. Share when you fail too. Create a culture where SDRs know that it's okay to fail, to learn a lesson from it, and to move on. This will help the SDRs on your team learn to be resilient.

3. It rewards SDRs. There are two ways you can reward SDRs with this contest. You can pay them a SPIFF when they beat you. You can also gift them the meetings you book and let it count towards their quota. They'll appreciate it. It's not like you are compensated for meetings.

4. You need the pipeline. If your team is struggling to hit their pipeline goals, you can give the team a boost. It helps you as well since you are most likely compensated and judged for overall team performance.

5. It's fun if you're crazy like me. There's nothing like showing your team that you've still got it. I was an SDR for 13 years. It's hard not to miss it. Plus, a little trash talking amongst the team can be fun.

Don't go in as if you must win every contest against your team. We know you're the team's leader for a reason. It's okay to take a dive for the sake of the team's morale.

Even outside of beat-the-boss contests, SDR Managers should continue outbounding on an abbreviated schedule. Making calls would be nice but you don't always have to include phone calls in your outbounding. You could leverage your professional connections on social media. You could also use your sales enablement platform to run automated-email sequences. (Although, it would be wise to follow up by phone with prospects who have multiple clicks and opens.) I'm not saying you need to go as far as carrying a quota but you should give yourself a daily KPI to hit.

Many SDR Managers will tell you that they don't want to do SDRs' jobs for them. If your team is struggling to hit its goals, and you're compensated and reviewed on their performance, you're really helping yourself. I don't know about you, but I like making more money and having job security.

Of course, you're busy. We're all busy. At the time of this writing, I manage SDR Managers. And guess what? I still prospect and book meetings for my teams. If I can find the time from the managers' manager chair, surely you can too. How about just 30 minutes a day?

Some SDR Managers will get distracted by their titles. *Doesn't this make me more of a player/coach than a manager?* Maybe, but who cares? You should never be above the job of the person you are leading. If you've ever watched the TV show called *The Profit*, you will see multi-millionaire investor, Marcus Lemonis, rolling up his sleeves and doing all the jobs the employees do. Why does he do it? He wants to walk a mile in the employees' shoes and learn the business from the inside out before he invests. It doesn't matter if he is mixing batter, sweeping floors, or shoveling dirt, he is never above doing the work.

SDR Managers need to be like Marcus Lemonis. Never be above doing the work, especially when it was the work that got you where you are today.

Speaking of work, some of the hardest work you'll ever do as a leader will be discussed in the next chapter. It's a part of leadership I still struggle with today. Turn to the next chapter to learn more.

Part 2

THE OTHER STUFF

Chapter 9

DATA SCIENTIST

I have a confession.

I hate researching data.

Spreadsheets make me want to puke.

Presenting that data to executive leadership? I'm all good if it's positive. But if it's negative, my stomach gets tied up in knots.

QBRs? Oh, brother.

In fact, even though you're not reading it last, I wrote this chapter last because I just don't love this stuff.

My lack of love for data started at Sinclair Community College in Dayton, Ohio while I was in the Air Force.

Throughout high school, I was a solid 3.5 GPA student. I was a math wiz. I even took and passed Advanced Placement Calculus. That was until I got accepted to Michigan State University. Afterwards, I got a bad case of Senioritis.

I thought I had arrived. I was already accepted at college of choice. Why did I need to keep trying so hard in high school?

The grades in my last semester of high school brought down my GPA. This also prompted a meeting with Michigan State. They wanted to ensure that I was going to be a good student.

I wasn't.

I arrived at MSU and partied like an animal. My fake ID made it easy to buy lots of booze. The ability to write raps had me performing in school talent shows thinking I was going to be the next L.L. Cool J. And since I rarely bothered to attend classes, I ended up living back at home in my mom's basement after only a year of college.

I joined the Air Force a couple of years later. When I got stationed at Wright-Patterson Air Force Base, I started taking courses at Sinclair Community College. Being a business major, I had to take three accounting courses. I figured since I was good at math, I could crush Accounting.

Nope.

I worked my tail off to get a "C" in every course. Spreadsheets. Balance sheets. Cash flow statements. I hated it all. I may not have known what I wanted to do after the Air Force, but I definitely knew I didn't want to be an accountant.

That disdain for data and spreadsheets stuck with me for a lifetime. Even as an entrepreneur, I avoided the accounting stuff like it was Covid-19.

Becoming an SDR Manager and then a director forced me into coming to terms with researching data and reporting it back up to executive leadership.

I still don't love it. But now I know enough about it to perform my job well.

As an SDR Manager, you'll be called upon to provide quarterly business reviews (QBRs), pipeline and forecast reports, and business cases to support purchasing the tools your team needs to exceed performance.

Let's start with the QBR.

QBRS

Many organizations expect their SDR leaders to provide a quarterly business review. A QBR is a report on your team's performance for the previous quarter. It may also contain an element of forecasting, especially if the previous quarter requires some course correction.

The QBR can be merely a slide deck presentation you send to executive leadership. However, most executive leaders expect you to provide an oral presentation along with the slides.

Depending on your audience, you may get through the entire presentation without interruption. My experience has been the opposite. Every leader is different, so many different leaders will key in on things that are most important to them.

Since many people absorb information more easily through pictures, it is important that you include charts and graphs to paint a picture.

No two SDR teams are the same. So, your QBR may look a little different than your colleague's QBR at another company. Heck, it may look different from your colleague's QBR at the same company. Regardless of that, there are a few elements of a QBR that are pretty standard.

HEADCOUNT

Executive leadership need to know the number of SDRs you have on your team. This allows you to put a face to all the names of your team. So make sure to include a picture of each team member. At one company, I found a picture of the first USA basketball dream team and replaced the players' faces with the faces of the SDRs on my team. It was a big hit!

Headcount shows if you have enough SDRs in seat to accomplish your qualified opportunities goals and pipeline goals.

If you've predetermined the ratio of SDRs needed to cover AEs, your headcount will show if all the AEs are covered or if you have hiring needs.

While discussing your team's headcount, it is important to include tenure and risk for attrition.

In this section, you can also highlight the individual teams the SDRs belong to, such as Inbound, Outbound, Small-to-Medium Sized Business (SMB), Mid-Market, Enterprise, Commercial, Government, or even vertical.

Outbound BDR Team		
Tenure	Name	Team
4.5 months	Jennifer Riley	SMB
11 months	Gabriel Little	SMB
2 years	Daniel Walker	Mid-Market
1.5 years	Tanya Wright	Mid-Market
9 months	Aimee Nichols	Enterprise
11 months	Rick Batista	Enterprise

Figure 9.1

PIPELINE AND QUALIFIED OPPORTUNITIES

The most important part of your QBR is going to be reporting on the team's performance in hitting their pipeline goals and qualified opportunities goals. There are a few ways you should display this data.

MONTH OVER MONTH PERFORMANCE

A month over month breakdown of the quarter gives your audience more microdata to view within the quarter. It also gives you the opportunity to highlight trends such as seasonal buying patterns, inbound marketing effectiveness, and hiring challenges.

A graphic representation of this data will make it easier to digest. Expect to add some color commentary as to why performance is up or down.

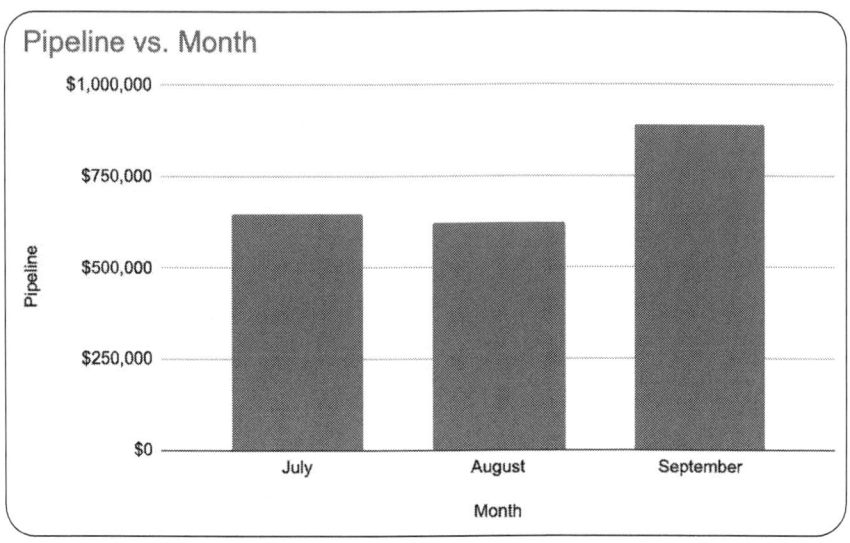

Figure 9.2

QUARTER OVER QUARTER PERFORMANCE

There are two ways to report your data quarter over quarter. You can report how the past quarter compared to the one before it. For example, you'd show how Q4 this year compared to Q3 this year.

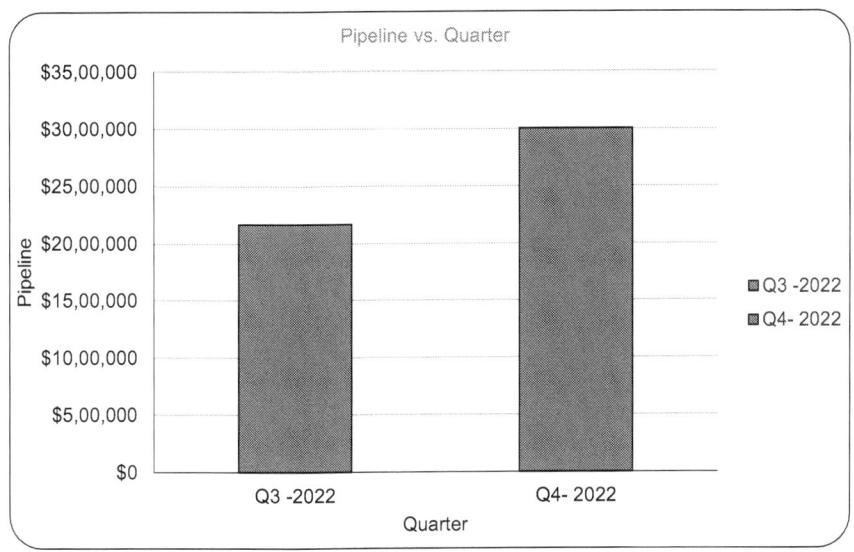

Figure 9.3

Or you can show how the past quarter compared to the same quarter a year ago. For example, you'd show how Q4 this year compared to Q4 last year.

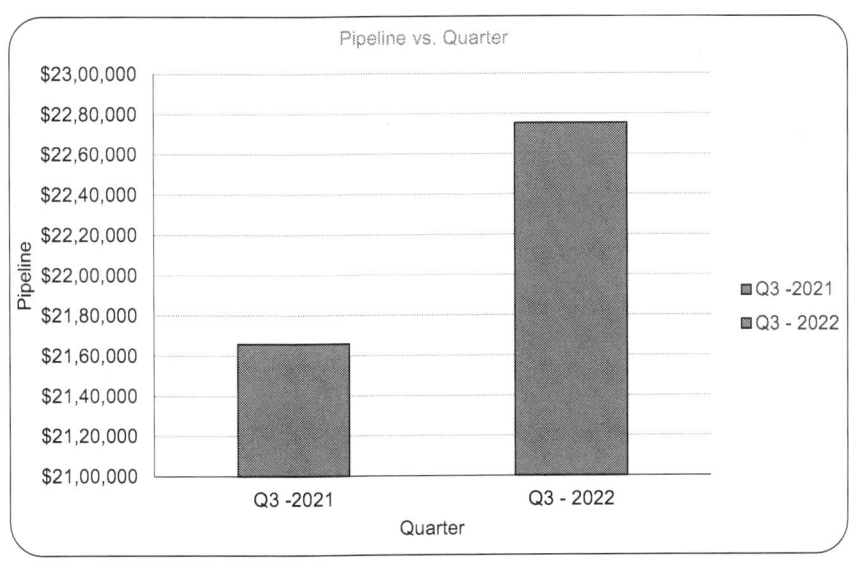

Figure 9.4

INDIVIDUAL PERFORMANCES

It's important to highlight the performance of all the individual SDRs on your team. You should also be prepared to share why SDRs are performing at a certain level.

Are they tenured or are they ramping?

Are they paired with experienced AEs or are the AEs new to the organization?

Do they have industry experience?

Do they have different work ethics?

Are they more skilled in cold calling than others?

Do they shine when booking meetings via email or social media?

Are they more efficient with their time?

Do they put in more activities than the rest of their team?

Outbound BDR Team				
Tenure	Name	Team	Goal	Attainment
4.5 months	Jennifer Riley	SMB	$150,000	$78,500
11 months	Gabriel Little	SMB	$150,000	$165,000
2 years	Daniel Walker	Mid-Market	$350,000	$360,000
1.5 years	Tanya Wright	Mid-Market	$350,000	$350,525
9 months	Aimee Nichols	Enterprise	$500,000	$745,350
11 months	Rick Batista	Enterprise	$500,000	$345,245

Figure 9.5

ACTIVITY REPORTS

More and more executive leaders are interested in SDRs' day-to-day activities. In fact, I was shocked to learn that the private equity firm that purchased the company I worked for was adamant about seeing this data. I thought they wouldn't be concerned with the minutiae of SDRs. Boy was I wrong.

Chances are, the SDRs on your team have a daily KPI that includes dials, emails, social media outreach, researching net new accounts, and more. It's important to share how each individual SDR did towards their daily KPI goal. It will look a lot cleaner if it shows the monthly or even quarterly goals versus performance.

For example, if the SDRs needed to make 50 dials over 20 workdays, you'd want to show how many dials out of 1000 they made for the month.

The results of your activity reports will reveal two things: Which SDRs are more efficient (getting more results with fewer activities) and which SDRs are putting forth the effort (hitting or exceeding daily activity goals).

Outbound BDR Team						
Name	Dials Goal	Attain-ment	Emails Goal	Attain-ment	Account Launch Goal	Attain-ment
Jennifer Riley	1000	849	500	525	100	103
Gabriel Little	1000	1005	500	495	100	97

Outbound BDR Team						
Daniel Walker	1000	925	500	503	100	100
Tanya Wright	1000	1257	500	745	100	115
Aimee Nichols	1000	1103	500	500	100	79
Rick Ba-tista	1000	723	500	275	100	54
Totals	6000	5862	3,000	3,043	600	548

Figure 9.6

When discussing activity metrics, it's important to call out any trends you're seeing such as:

- Connect rates (On average, how many prospects pick up the phone?)
- Open rates (How emails are being opened?)
- Clickthrough rates (How many prospects open links within emails?)
- Webinar registrations versus attendees
- Show rates (How many prospects are ghosting SDRs for meetings?)

SUCCESS METRICS

While creating pipeline and qualified opportunities is the primary goal of SDRs, the reason SDR teams exist is to create pipeline that becomes Closed Won deals. In other words, revenue.

That's why it is important to track SDR-generated pipeline all the way to closing. In your QBR, you definitely want to highlight the amount of revenue generated from SDR pipeline. You should also highlight the net new business (logos) your team helped to generate. If a Chief Revenue Officer or Chief Sales Officer is in your audience, this will be the most important data to share.

Don't worry if there aren't many Closed Won deals. This is especially true if your team has done its job in hitting its pipeline goals and qualified opportunities goals. The lack of closed won deals should help the CRO or CSO better understand how AEs are managing SDR-generated pipeline.

Outbound BDR Team					
Tenure	Name	Team	Goal	Attainment	Closed Won
4.5 months	Jennifer Riley	SMB	$150,000	$78,500	$10,550
11 months	Gabriel Little	SMB	$150,000	$165,000	$24,500
2 years	Daniel Walker	Mid-Market	$350,000	$360,000	$80,500
1.5 years	Tanya Wright	Mid-Market	$350,000	$350,525	$155,450
9 months	Aimee Nichols	Enter-prise	$500,000	$745,350	$125,000
11 months	Rick Batista	Enter-prise	$500,000	$345,245	$40,000
Totals			$2,000,000	$2,044,620	$436,000

Figure 9.7

SEQUENCES, CADENCES, OR SALES PLAYS

If you are running multiple sequences, cadences, or sales plays, it is important to highlight the ones that helped generate the most meetings.

In the case of inbound sequences (webinar follow-up, content follow-up, etc.) highlighting these can help to determine if it makes sense to invest more in the resources that generated the inbound leads.

PERSONAS OR TITLES OF MEETING TAKERS

Do the people who take meetings most have a certain job? Are they at a certain level? For example, do IT Managers take more meetings than CIOs?

In your QBR, you should highlight the titles and levels of prospects that have taken meetings over the quarter. This will not only help your audience see who is interested in what you sell but it will help you determine who to target moving forward.

INDUSTRIES

What industries have prospects been in who take meetings? Are they in manufacturing, IT, finance, or something else? Are you able to isolate the top three industries?

That's the type of data that needs to go into your QBR. These trends help to determine future plays, sequences, and forecasts.

FORECAST

I get it. You are no Nostradamus. However, based on headcount, seasonality, and past performance, you should be able to provide a forecast of how you think your team will perform next quarter. Chart it out. Highlight why you believe they will or will not hit their number. Talk about which cadences you plan to run, which titles or personas SDRs will pursue, and what additional training and coaching you will provide to make it happen.

Note that in many organizations, discussing quarter-to-date performance and your forecast happens more than quarterly. I've worked for companies that required SDR leadership to provide weekly updates on pipeline, performance, and outcomes.

APPENDIX

Although QBRs have an element of presenting data to your audience, there simply won't be enough time to present all the data.

That's why when it comes to the micro-level data, you'll want to add that to the appendix of your QBR slides. Day-to-day data, annual month over month performance, and more should be documented and added to the appendix.

A good way to determine what information should go into the appendix is to put yourself in your audience's shoes. What information might they ask you more details about?

Instead of adding actual charts, graphs, and reports to the appendix, make them available via links. Link to your CRM, your sales enablement platform, and to Excel reports outside of your QBR slides.

The appendix lets your audience know that you have the correct data and that you've done your homework. Plus, you just never know when someone may ask you for it.

BUSINESS CASES

You'll need to write up a business case when you want to buy software or a service for your team. Here's the thing about them. You win some. You lose some. Throughout my career, I can say that 40% of my business cases were shut down. Either there was no budget, or the budget was allocated for something else. Or the business case didn't prove enough return on investment, especially after executive leadership poked holes in it.

I'm proud to say that I was able to help my teams get Outreach, VoiceReach (an auto-dialer), Reachdesk (a gifting platform), and LeadIQ (a contact database for finding business and mobile phone numbers). Had it not been for my ability to write a business case, we wouldn't have purchased these platforms.

Not only did these tools help our productivity but they also helped the team I led to recognize me as a leader who had their success at heart.

To write a successful business case, your report should include a few elements:

- Vendor's Company Information and History
- Top 3 Competitors of the Vendor and Why They Were Not Selected (Do Your Due Diligence)
- Forecasted ROI in Pipeline, Opportunities, and Revenue if Purchased (Tables and Charts)
- Pros and Cons of the Vendor
- Opportunity Costs (What happens if we don't buy.)
- Pricing, Support, and Implementation Costs
- Security (of the software)
- Customer Testimonials and Case Studies
- Links to Product Reviews
- Links to Demos and Product Sheets

Chapter 10

DIPLOMAT

If your organization is large enough, you may have the privilege of working with other teams. These teams usually support Sales. Among those teams might be Demand Generation, which usually sits under the Marketing team. You may also have a Sales Enablement team and a Sales Operations team. However, the most important team to be in lockstep with is the folks who manage the closers (AKA account executives). Let's look at each team in relation to your SDR team.

AES

Having a great relationship with the account executives and their managers is crucial. AEs are your internal customers. Without them, SDRs would have no one to create meetings and pipeline for. Oftentimes, AEs have the power to determine if SDRs have given them a qualified lead or unqualified lead. In the SDR world, qualified leads determine the greatest portion of commission checks.

As a leader responsible for providing a specific number of meetings and pipeline per quarter, you'll want to make sure AEs are satisfied with the quality of leads your team provides. Not only does it make sense for the SDRs on your team to meet regularly with the AEs they support, but it's equally important that you meet with their leaders to discuss the success of the SDR program.

Program. The function of the SDR team is a program. Make no mistake about it. Not only is it a program but the success of the program is often determined by the AE team. If AEs are not closing more in revenue than the cost of the program (your salary and your team's salaries), it can be considered a failed program. It doesn't matter if your team is researching the right contacts, BANT qualifying their prospects, and overdelivering in meetings and pipeline. No return on investment equals a failed program.

That's why SDR leaders have got to get this relationship right. You need to work with AE leaders to agree upon what a qualified lead is. You might even get it in writing in a Service-Level Agreement (SLA).

You have got to work with AE leaders to determine the deadline for AEs to convert a meeting to a qualified opportunity. An SLA comes in handy here too.

You've got to gauge the relationship between SDRs and AEs to ensure AEs are happy. If there are personality clashes or if there is underperformance, it's up to you to remedy that situation.

And that is when you put on your diplomat hat.

In my third year as an SDR at a digital marketing firm, I was paired with two AEs. One AE was great. He was experienced. He had industry knowledge. He treated me like a partner, not his assistant. Above all this, he closed deals.

On the other hand, that other AE was horrible. He treated me like an assistant. He walked around like he was the king of the world. Worst of all, in two years of employment, he didn't close a single deal. I'm not talking just the qualified meetings I provided. I'm talking about his own warm leads and referrals, leads from live events, and more.

As an SDR, I overperformed to the point that my one-month earned commission check had to be spread out over three months.

One month after I had gotten a raise for my performance, my team was laid off.

While I may have been crushing it as an SDR, that AE was not. As a program, the SDR team was a failure. Perhaps if I had a diplomat leader in the background advocating for me, I may have not been laid off.

DEMAND GENERATION

Demand Generation professionals are primarily responsible for helping to generate inbound leads and pipeline. The types of inbound leads they generate include demo requests, free trial requests, webinar registrations, live event registrations, and content downloads (such as e-books or blog posts).

Many Demand Generation teams have their own pipeline goals. More often, their pipeline goals are blended with your SDR team's goals, especially if you have a stand-alone Inbound team. Because your team's success is dependent on the Demand Generation team's success, it is super important that you communicate regularly with them.

When I worked for an emergency alerting software company, I met weekly with the folks on the Demand Gen team. We collaborated on cadences, as they would often write the email copy. They shared with me what they were doing to drive inbound leads like planning and executing webinars, creating blog posts, and working with affiliates to generate leads. I shared with them what was working, what wasn't working, and what ideas could work to generate more leads.

The important thing was that we kept a weekly cadence. We even had a special name for our combined teams, the Smarketing team. (Sales + Marketing + smart).

The relationship wasn't all puppy dogs and ice cream. We had our contentious moments. When Demand Generation worked hard on creating, promoting, and delivering a highly attended webinar but SDRs didn't follow up, that was an issue. When Inbound SDRs expected 400 inbound leads per month and only received 280 in July, that was an issue. Or when SDRs were waiting on a new sequence that allowed them to easily follow up with event attendees, it was an issue for all of us.

That's where the diplomat comes in. As a leader, it is your job to smooth the relationship between your team and the Demand Generation team. That means being accountable for your team's mistakes. It means showing up for all of the scheduling meetings and fully participating. It also means making the Demand Gen team feel valuable.

Besides giving a lot of "thank yous" to that team, I leveraged our internal rewards system to show my appreciation. You may have a rewards program like Bonusly or Kudos that allows you to publicly acknowledge your fellow employees while allowing them to earn points towards gift cards. While we as managers are good at using those platforms to reward the teams we lead, we often forget to use them to reward those across other teams when they support us.

SALES ENABLEMENT

Sales Enablement is an important team to use your diplomatic skills on as well. They onboard, train, and reinforce the training your SDRs receive. They uncover the best personas, best industries, and ideal customer profiles (ICPs) to pursue. They evaluate and purchase learning management systems (LMS). If you have a Sales Enablement team, don't take them for granted. They take a lot of the training and onboarding off your plate so that you can focus on other important things. Believe me. I've worked for organizations where there was no Sales Enablement team. That meant I was responsible for creating buyer personas, creating and executing onboarding and training, and reinforcing that training through coaching.

It's important to establish a regular cadence of meetings with your Sales Enablement team as well. In those meetings, you can discuss what training and onboarding is working. You can review buyer personas, Ideal Customer Profiles (ICPs), and verticals SDRs are reaching out to. You can also collaborate on any new training you'd like your team to go through. For example, I worked with my Sales Enablement team to create a training program with quizzes and a certification on how to personalize their outreach. We also collaborated on how to leverage personalized videos and texting in our outbound process.

Don't forget to show your appreciation of the Sales Enablement folks. A little Bonusly, Kudos, or even a $10 Starbucks gift card can go a long way.

SALES OPERATIONS

You can even be a diplomat with your Sales Operations team. They are the folks who have a strong input on the software you'll need for your team. Sales Operations are often the people maintaining that software, such as your CRM, your sales enablement platform, and your researchable contact database. Some Sales Operations teams will even import data from your contact database to your CRM for you.

They are essential. While you may not need to meet with them as regularly as you would Demand Generation or Sales Enablement, it is still important to use your diplomatic skills with them. Ask how you can help them. Get their advice on purchasing the software you want. Acknowledge and reward them when they help members of your team to solve a problem.

Being a diplomat is not limited to AE teams, Demand Generation, Sales Enablement, and Sales Operations. You may find yourself working for an organization with a Customer Success team. Those are the folks responsible for upsells to the existing client base.

On occasion, an SDR may accidentally reach out to an existing client. If your team is not in an expansion model where they could contact existing clients, that might result in some harsh words from your Customer Success Managers (CSMs). It's just another occasion to put on your diplomat hat and take accountability for your team's mistake. And if the CSM is nice about the situation, why not send out a reward to keep the peace?

The main thing I want you to take away from this chapter is that there are many facets to the SDR Manager job. It's important to understand all the key players within your organization and how they affect your ability to successfully do your job. Oftentimes, that means stepping out of the manager/coach role and being a diplomat and colleague with those other teams.

When I was applying for my first full-time SDR Manager job, a friend of mine recommended I read a book called The First 90 Days by Michael Watkins. It's an excellent resource that will help you further along in your journey as a diplomat within your organization.

If you don't have a Demand Generation team or if you have a small Marketing team, you'll have to do some of the marketing yourself. The next chapter will help.

Chapter 11

MARKETER

If you came up from an SDR role into leadership, you'll better understand that the SDR role is the intersection of sales and marketing. It's not 100% sales. It's not 100% marketing.

SDRs perform sales tasks like researching prospects, cold calling, sending cold emails, booking first meetings, and even running discovery calls. However, SDRs do not negotiate terms, run demos, or collaborate with internal Legal and Finance teams. Above all, they don't close deals. They are not exactly telemarketers. Although they use the phone (email and social too) to market a product or service. They don't do one-call closes like a business-to-customer (B2C) rep does.

SDRs perform marketing duties too like posting on social media, crafting their own emails, and sometimes writing their own cadences.

To add to the confusion, SDRs might report to Sales, or they might report to Marketing. (My personal belief is that if you've never made cold calls for a living, you shouldn't be leading an SDR team.)

Sometimes Inbound SDRs report to Marketing and Outbound SDRs report to Sales. As an SDR and an SDR leader, I have reported to Marketing and to Sales.

If you came up as an SDR, you'll know that part of the job is doing marketing work. Although you probably won't be responsible for creating beautifully written e-books, blog posts, or one-sheeters, you will be accountable for writing email templates, call scripts and sequences. (You may be asked to share social posts too.)

This chapter is focused on emails and sequences.

Let me start by saying if your writing skills and grammar skills are not up to par, you should download a free version of Grammarly. This grammar-checking software will save you from embarrassment and heartache. Have the SDRs on your team download it too.

EMAIL

If you don't have the luxury of a Demand Generation team or a Marketing team to help you craft emails, you're on your own. If you don't have a clue on how to write good email copy, consider taking a course through sites like Udemy, Coursera, or LinkedIn Learning. There are some great copywriting books out there as well.

SUBJECT LINES

Subject lines are an important part of writing email copy. After all, if the email doesn't get opened, it won't get read. And certainly, prospects will not take action on unread emails.

In your emails, I highly suggest including the prospect's first name in the subject line. We're naturally drawn to our own names. Plus, it appears the email may be personalized just for that prospect.

Consider adding a known problem your company solves that your prospect might have in the subject line. An example might be: Hannah - Improve customer satisfaction with this...

Many marketing gurus swear by asking a question in the subject line to create intrigue. For example: Joe - Did you make quota this month?

If you have a sales enablement platform like Outreach or Salesloft, you can A/B test your subject lines. Experiment with two different subject lines. Send out 100 emails. Then look at the open rates to determine which subject line yields the most opens. Once you determine a winner, you can turn off the template with the poorer results.

If you decide to A/B test subject lines, make sure the body of both emails are identical. That way, there is no confusion on what's prompting opens. Some email systems allow you to see a preview of the body of the email.

EMAIL BODY

There are just a few tips I want to share with you regarding the body of your emails.

The first tip is to create short paragraphs. They shouldn't be more than two sentences. A software platform like Lavender can help you with this.

Secondly, make the body of the emails short enough to be read on a mobile phone without scrolling.

Next, use actionable salutations in the signature. Don't use "Best" or "Thanks." Instead, let the prospect know you're expecting them to act. My favorites are, "Thanks in advance," "Let me know," and "Looking forward to hearing back."

Finally, deliverability is key. You want emails to reach the Inbox not the Spam folder. So, avoid sending links in the first email. Avoid bullet points in first emails too. And never send an attachment unless it has been requested.

ON PERSONALIZATION

Nobody wants to feel like a number. Email personalization allows your SDRs to make prospects feel special. When an email is only relevant to one prospect, that is when you know your SDRs are doing personalization right.

There are several ways to personalize an email.

You can find something you have in common with the prospect and include it.

You can find something interesting about the prospect and write about it.

You may read something in the news about the prospect's company that is relative to what you sell and include it.

You might find something the prospect posted online, read it, and comment about it in your email.

If you subscribe to the prospect's company newsletter, you are bound to find something worth mentioning.

You may even discover that a prospect attended a specific event that you can reference.

While I am a huge fan of personalizing emails, there is a cost associated with them.

Time.

It takes way more time to research prospects and find ways to incorporate what you learned in an email. And sometimes the juice is not worth the squeeze. Imagine taking 30 minutes to research a prospect and crafting the perfect email only for the email to not get opened, to go to the Spam folder, or to just bounce.

One of my favorite experts on email personalization is Becc Holland, the CEO of Flip the Script. You can find several her training videos on how to personalize at scale on YouTube.

At one company, we made one of her training videos mandatory for SDRs to view. They are *that* good.

INDUSTRY STANDARDS

If your emails are yielding a 23% or greater open rate, you're doing well.

If your emails are yielding between 7% and 10% reply rates, you're doing well. (Your sales enablement platform will even help you determine positive replies versus negative.)

If your emails are yielding between 1% and 2% clickthroughs, you are doing well.

If your emails are not yielding these results, you've got some tinkering to do. Your A/B testing can help. Change the body of the email. Change the content you're linking to. And yes, change the subject line. Just do these things one at a time. If you change all things at once, you won't be able to determine what was successful and what wasn't.

Everyone is selling something different to different industries to different personas. Because of this, I'm purposely avoiding telling you what specifically to write in your emails. Instead, I encourage you to Google the top books on copywriting and choose one to read. You can also find more tips for writing prospecting emails in my book, *Brain Dump*.

SEQUENCES (OR CADENCES)

Outreach calls them sequences. Salesloft calls them cadences. All in all, they are sequential steps the SDRs on your team take in the attempt to book time with a prospect.

As an SDR Manager, it is your job to write them. Not Marketing. Not Demand Generation. Not SDRs.

Yours.

Writing cadences is an important job. Getting the data on the results of those cadences is equally important.

If you are blessed to have historical data on which tasks create the most meetings, you can use it to determine your sequence steps. Steps can include:

- Phone call
- Manual Email
- Auto-Email
- Social media connection request
- Direct message on social media
- Send personalized video
- Text
- Direct mail
- Email with an electronic gift card
- Venmo (Send two cents and tell the prospects you'd like to give them your two cents on how you can help them.)

If responses to emails yield twice the meetings as phone conversations, for example, you will want to have more emails in your cadence than phone calls. If personalized videos in emails result in more responses than emails with text, you'll want to have your SDRs sending personalized videos first.

INTERVALS

The intervals between steps are important as well. Should your SDRs call, email, and send a LinkedIn connection request on the first day? Or should they space out each of these steps over one or two days?

As a best practice, most SDR Managers space out the steps over two or three days. And SDRs rarely have more than two steps per day. If SDRs have three or more steps in a sequence on the same day, they are most likely to skip steps.

Another best practice is to combine steps whenever you can. For example, if SDRs should view the prospect's LinkedIn page before making a phone call, don't make those two different steps. Instead, add the LinkedIn viewing instructions on the call step.

SAMPLE CADENCE

Here is what a sample cadence looks like:
Day 1 - Auto-Email (A/B test two subject lines)
Day 3 – View LinkedIn profile then Phone Call - personalized voicemail
Day 4 - Auto-Email Reply to First Email

Day 5 - Send LinkedIn Connection Request

Day 7 - Phone Call – voicemail drop message

Day 9 - Send Personalized Video Email

Day 10 - Phone Call (hang up and immediately dial again if no answer)

Day 12 - Manual Personalized Email

Day 15 - Text

Day 16 - Phone Call – voicemail drop from internal same title

Day 17 - Auto-Email with gift card offer

Day 20 – Venmo – send two cents

The outcomes from your first cadence will help you to craft better ones in the future. You'll be able to determine the average number of steps it takes to book a meeting. You'll also learn which subject line works best. Which task results in more meetings booked will be revealed as well. From there, you iterate until you have a group of high-performing cadences.

SEQUENCE ORGANIZATION

Keeping tabs on your sequences is not a big deal when you are first starting out. When you start to create hundreds of sequences and SDRs clone versions of those sequences, it can be a nightmare to keep them organized. One organization I worked with had over 1800 active sequences.

To keep your sequences organized, you need to incorporate tags and naming conventions.

Tags are simply names associated with your sequences to make them easier to find. For example, if you manage Inbound SDRs and Outbound SDRs, you may want to tag your sequences either Inbound or Outbound.

The way you title your sequences make them easier to keep up with too. For example, if my team attended the Retail Marketers' conference every year and we used sequences to follow up, I might title my sequences: Retail Marketers' January 2022 Follow Up. That way, SDRs won't add prospects to the previous years' sequences that have different messaging and different steps.

Adding the correct tags and naming conventions to your sequences is worth the time.

At one company where I was the SDR Manager, my teams were segmented by government, commercial, and education. I partnered with our Demand Generation team to create three different sequences for one event.

Although the language in the emails were similar, there were distinctions. Colleges called their "customers" students. Governments did not call their organizations companies. And companies didn't call their employees "residents." When SDRs mixed up which sequences to use, there was some negative backlash.

BLUEPRINTS

If you are totally lost on where to start on writing cadences, no need to worry. Many of the sales enablement platforms come with blueprints that show you what tasks and what intervals work best in certain industries. When it comes to writing email copy, you are on your own.

WHY USE SALES ENABLEMENT PLATFORMS?

If you have a sales enablement platform in place, consider it a luxury. There are still organizations who don't believe in them or simply don't have the budget for them.

I remember a time when I worked as an independent contractor. The company I worked for did not want to shell out the money for a CRM like Salesforce. Instead, they used a juiced-up Excel program. It was horrible.

Another company I worked for did not adapt to using a sales enablement platform even though the SEPs were becoming wildly popular. Instead, their CRM was their sales enablement platform and Quick Parts within Microsoft Word was used for email. They were way behind in the times. Last I heard that is still the case in 2022.

There are four reasons I love sales enablement platforms:

1. **Pre-recorded voicemails -** The SDRs on your team can pre-record their more generic messages. When the prospect's voicemail greeting kicks in, the SDRs can just click a button to leave a message. That eliminates SDRs wasting their time and their voices on leaving the same message over and over again. Those first messages, however, should be personalized and left live.

2. **Metrics** - You as a manager can easily see which team members are keeping up with their required daily activities such as dials and emails. You can also view connect rates, the number of prospects actively being reached out to, and a lot more.

3. **Email Opens** - When emails are opened more than once, it prompts SDRs to know there is interest or that the prospect is forwarding the email. Either way, the SDR should make calling the prospect a priority over the ones who have not opened emails. Seeing the clicks and replies are cool too. For SDR Managers, they can read the objections SDRs are receiving and how (or if) SDRs are handling objections over email. Too many SDR Managers new to the role neglect to provide coaching on email replies.

4. **Recorded Calls** - Recorded conversations make coaching so much easier. Recordings allow you to distinguish between SDRs having real conversations versus just leaving voicemails. Sales enablement platforms allow you to write coaching notes at the moment of the call you are talking about. Many of the sales enablement platforms allow you to listen live and coach live. However, listening live can be a waste of time when the majority of calls result in leaving a voicemail. And coaching in real time can be a distraction for SDRs.

REPORTS

As I said earlier, reports within your sales enablement platform are just as important as writing cadences. When you put on your data scientist hat and report that data back up to executive leadership, you will value the reports even more.

Reports will help you to determine:
- The times prospects are most likely to answer the phone
- The sequences that result in the most meetings booked
- The number of steps it takes to book a meeting in sequence
- Dials to connects rates
- Connect rates to meetings booked rates
- Email performance
- Top-performing SDRs
- And more...

WORKING OUTSIDE OF CADENCES

Cadences are great for structure, but they can also stagnate a more creative SDR. If your cadence steps don't incorporate every technology imaginable, you should give the SDRs you trust the freedom to experiment.

Outbounding is not just about calls and emails anymore. Does your cadence include a Vidyard personalized video step? How about a TikTok challenge step? What about a text with a link to a recorded customer testimonial on G2?

Prospects love video. When a salesperson sends me a video, I hit Play 99% of the time. Emails with text only? Not so much. So why don't more SDRs use personalized videos?

I had a lot of success getting meetings by sending prospects 60-second video presentations. It was just a video of me showing a couple of slides. If you're not emphasizing the usage of video in your team's outbounding, the SDRs on your team will figure it out and do it themselves.

Do you coach your team to use LinkedIn voice messages?

Can SDRs slide into your prospects' Instagram DMs?

What about sending those two cents to their prospects on Venmo?

Do they ever mail a coffee mug with their prospect's college logo on it?

These tactics are worth a shot if they help the SDRs on your team get their prospects' attention. It's even more worth it if reps book meetings from these outside- of-the-box methods.

Cadences are wonderful for keeping SDRs on task, creating efficiency, and lowering the chances of them making a mistake. You should still leave some wiggle room for creativity and experimentation.

Ask the SDRs on your team about the most creative ways they've booked meetings. You might hear something the whole team can use.

SOCIAL MEDIA PROMOTER

As the leader of the SDR team, you may be charged with posting information about your company on social media. While tweets and LinkedIn posts are not as labor-intensive as writing sequences with A/B testing templates, they can be a task, nonetheless.

Regardless of the allowed characters on social media platforms, it's important to keep your messages short. Most of us are scrolling through our feed. We really don't have time to read any dissertations.

Chances are, you won't be tasked with posting a bunch of original content. Instead, you'll be asked to comment on or share the content created by your Demand Generation or Marketing team. (Gotta love those folks.)

Here are a few Dos and Don'ts when it comes to sharing your company's content on LinkedIn:

Do:
- Use hashtags
- Like or comment on the post on your company's page
- Share your company's post
- Incentivize your team for sharing posts
- Post links in the comment section of your shared post
- Engage with prospects that engage with your content

Don't:

- Make sharing posts a requirement for your team. (You don't own their personal accounts.)
- Add links in the body of the posts. (It will be flagged by the algorithm and shared less.)
- Forget to view which companies are engaging with your content
- Write a dissertation. Be brief.
- Forget to check your spelling and grammar
- Engage with negative commenters

Look at you. You're becoming a straight up marketing guru. Add a few search engine optimization and search engine marketing classes. Next thing you know, you're the new VP of Demand Generation.

Before that, it's important to be prepared to plan events for your team and strategize on which events your team will attend. If you are ready to get started, turn to the next page.

Chapter 12

EVENT PLANNER

There are two types of events you'll need to plan for your SDR team: professional and social. Let's start with the professional events.

PROFESSIONAL

The SDR role is the intersection between sales and marketing. That makes them the perfect employees to attend live trade shows.

Trade shows are typically planned by professional membership organizations, government organizations, or companies. They center on a common theme. They have large sessions and breakout sessions led by the organizations' employees or by guest speakers.

There are also booths for vendors. These are spaces set aside for organizations to grab the attention of the trade show audience.

The booths themselves may contain tables, computers, monitors, signage, company merchandise, swag to give away, games, snacks, and more. The goal is to create a space that will cause the audience to stop and take notice.

Naturally, you would want your most knowledgeable employees at those booths to answer questions, initiate conversations, and ultimately turn the audience into prospects. That's what makes SDRs the perfect candidates for running your trade show booths.

Essentially, SDRs do the same things at trade show booths that they do in their day-to-day jobs in the office or working remotely. They create interest. Initiate conversations. Ask qualifying questions. Offer gifts. Turn people into prospects.

When your organization includes employees with more product knowledge at these events (like AEs or sales engineers) SDRs can even set up on-the-spot discovery meetings and demos.

Given the monotony of the SDR role, most SDRs jump at the opportunity to attend live trade shows. That's because they get to travel. The company pays for their food, lodging, and transportation. They get to meet new people.

Most importantly, they get to prospect in person. It is 100% easier to prospect when you are in the same room than when you are using cold outbounding tactics.

Because SDRs like to attend trade shows, you can leverage this to your advantage. You can make having the right to attend a trade show contingent upon a micro-promotion. For example, if you have levels one, two, and three within the SDR role, you can require them to be a level two or a level three to be eligible.

If you don't have micro-promotions, you can turn the right to attend the trade show into a contest. This was my go-to tactic when I led a team at an Atlanta-based marketing technology firm. Whoever booked the most qualified meetings for the month got to attend trade shows in Charlotte, Orlando, and Detroit. We had record-breaking meetings and pipeline in those months too.

Because SDRs on my team were working for a software company for the first time, I attended a couple of these trade shows with them to show them the ropes. Plus, it was a nice getaway for me too. Of course, it would have been a lot nicer if the events were in Hawaii or Europe.

Even though the SDRs on my team saw attending these trade shows as a privilege worth working hard for, the truth was that we needed them there. The folks who normally attended the trade shows like the AEs, product marketing managers, and sales engineers were unavailable. Our Chief Revenue Officer tasked me with finding SDRs to attend. Making it a contest helped us build more pipeline and provide coverage for the shows.

There is a lot of planning that goes into participating in trade shows.

Ideally, you will want a list of registered attendees before the show starts. If your company sponsors the event, there is a good chance that you can get such a list. Once the list is secured, the SDRs on your team can start reaching out to attendees to schedule live meetings for the AEs attending.

You will also want the SDRs and other employees attending to meet to discuss their game plan. In this meeting, you can determine who will be responsible for shipping the booth materials, who will be setting up the booth, who will attend sessions, how the leads will get captured, who is going to run in-the-booth demos, what swag will be given away, and who is going to take down the booth.

For SDRs attending a trade show for the first time, it is a good practice to have them set up and take down your trade show display beforehand. Putting up banners, hooking up cords to monitors and keyboards, and setting up tablecloths and merchandise takes practice. If you don't have an AE or marketing employee to help, this will likely fall on your shoulders.

Virtual trade shows gained popularity during the Covid-19 pandemic. However, they weren't nearly as well-attended.

SOCIAL

Regardless of if your SDR team is working remotely or in the office, they need time for fun. The day-to-day grind of the job warrants time for planned fun activities.

You can use fun activities simply to allow SDRs to get away from it all (which actually reduces turnover). Or you can use fun activities to drive specific behaviors.

I've done it both ways.

When our marketing organization needed the SDR team to update thousands of records in our CRM, I turned it into a pizza party.

When I needed a strong, qualified meetings month, I promised my team a bowling party if every individual on the team hit 100% of quota. You should have seen how the top performers were helping the bottom performers. It was a thing of beauty. And the bowling party they won, complete with free beer and free food, was the talk of the office.

When my fully remote team was feeling burned out, I organized a virtual escape room event.

I have even organized happy hours that included in-person karaoke or virtual lip sync battles.

If you decide to organize fun activities for your team, don't assume they like what you like. Use a platform like SurveyMonkey to survey your team. Give them a list of events to choose from and ask them which would be the most fun and the most rewarding.

There are many other events you can plan for your team.

You could have an offsite bootcamp for team building.

You could have a scavenger hunt.

How about a holiday party with an ugliest sweater contest?

You could meetup at a sales-related trade show that helps them to further their sales education.

You could ask each rep to cook a dish and have a potluck lunch.

Have a designated day to wear specific clothing to work like a sports jersey day.

The possibilities are endless.

Being the designated event planner will help you stand out as a leader. More importantly, it will help your team feel less burned out and more like a cohesive unit. Because, trust me, disputes will happen.

If you need some ideas on how to settle disputes between SDRs and between SDRs and AEs, turn to the next chapter.

Chapter 13

REFEREE

As an SDR Manager, you are bound to have disputes on your team. These disputes can run the gamut. Some sample disputes include:

- Prospecting into someone else's territory and booking a meeting
- Another rep getting credit for someone else's work
- AEs disqualifying meetings that should be qualified
- And more...

The easiest way to deal with disputes before they even happen is to put the rules and requirements in writing. This can be done in your SDR playbook. It can also be written in a Service-Level Agreement (SLA) or in a Rules of Engagement (ROE) document.

SLAS

A service-level agreement is a written contract of which the terms are agreed upon by two parties. Internally, they usually apply to teams that work together but report to different departments.

For example, your Marketing team may write an SLA that states they will provide a minimum of 50 inbound demo requests per week to your Inbound SDR team. When your Inbound team is unable to hit quota because the Marketing team did not adhere to the SLA, it gives you a valid reason for not hitting team goals and a valid reason to temporarily lower your team's quotas.

The most common usage of an SLA comes with the SDR/AE relationship. Since the SDR technically serves the AE, it is the SDR team that provides the SLA.

Most of the time, the SLA is written by the SDR Manager. It can also be crafted jointly with the person who manages the AEs your team serves.

A classic case of using an SLA is when determining the minimum standard for SDRs to hand over a lead to an AE. Essentially, this conversation will revolve around qualification criteria. Some examples of qualification criteria include:

Budget, Authority, Need, and Timeline (B.A.N.T.) - In other words, if the SDR cannot find out the prospect's budget, need, authority to buy what you sell, and when they are looking to buy, the lead can be deemed unqualified.

Other SLAs are not as strict. At one outsourced business development firm, the SDRs were only required to uncover an interest and get a prospect who held a manager or above title to agree to a meeting.

This qualification criteria is one of my favorites. Think about it. SDRs are the most junior salespeople on your team. Do you really want them conducting mini-discovery calls with high-level executives? Chances are that those executives will have questions of their own that SDRs can't answer.

Authority and Interest (A.I.) - My favorite qualification criteria is what I like to call A.I. Let SDRs research the right people in an organization who have the authority to influence a buying decision. And let SDRs create enough interest that prospects want to have a longer conversation with someone who is more of a subject matter expert.

Some organizations only want their AEs having conversations with people who have a director title or above.

Some organizations require prospects to agree upon a specific challenge, pain, or use case before deeming them qualified.

Other companies look at firmographic information such as company size, number of employees, website traffic, or business software in place.

Regardless of what you decide a qualified lead looks like, the main point is to get it in writing in an SLA and to have all SDRs and AEs sign off on it.

AES' SLAS FOR SDRS

What about a service-level commitment from AEs to SDRs? There are a few cases when an SLA is needed. The main one is a minimum time to convert a meeting into a qualified opportunity.

Many AEs are notoriously horrible at flipping meetings to qualified opportunities in a timely manner. This is especially true if they are held accountable for closing a certain number of handoffs from SDRs, if they are disorganized, or if they are just bad at closing deals.

Though many AEs value the meetings and pipeline SDRs provide, they sometimes forget how SDRs get paid. The majority of SDRs are paid for providing qualified meetings. Most SDRs are paid commission monthly.

That's why it is important for AEs to have a timeline to convert meetings to qualified opportunities. My personal favorite is a minimum of two business days. But at the end of the month, AEs need to flip meetings to opps sooner.

The AEs who were promoted from SDR roles tend to be a lot better at flipping meetings to opps in a timely manner. For the rest of them, you'll need an SLA.

Without an SLA in place, you will be spending a lot of your days in reactive mode. Slack from SDRs. Emails from AEs. Zoom calls with your boss. Save yourself some time and headaches by putting some SLAs in place.

RULES OF ENGAGEMENT

While SLAs are more appropriate for disagreements between different teams, rules of engagement are more appropriate for disputes within the same team.

Some of the most common disputes within teams are:
- Inbound v. Outbound Disputes
- Inbound v. Inbound and Outbound v. Outbound Disputes

Bottom line: Everyone wants what they were promised, and no one wants their hard work to benefit someone else (especially when we are talking money and promotions).

However, SDRs will step on each other's toes. Sometimes it is intentional. Other times, it is purely accidental. Regardless of the intent, written rules of engagement can help you to settle many of your internal disputes.

Here are things to consider writing rules of engagement for:
- How long does an SDR have to reach out to a prospect before losing it?
- Who gets inbound leads?
- Which SDRs get which inbound leads? What's the criteria?
- What happens if an SDR books a qualified meeting on an account that belongs to another SDR? Who gets the credit? What if the account owning SDR never communicated with any of the prospects?
- How long does an Inbound SDR have to reach an inbound lead before losing it?
- What if the SDR knows someone at a prospective company but the lead is in another SDR's name?
- What happens to their leads after an SDR leaves your team?

- What happens if an Outbound SDR is outbounding to a contact at a company but another contact at the company becomes an inbound lead? Who gets credit for the inbound lead?
- When can SDRs reach out to existing customers if they can at all?
- When can SDRs reach out to prospects on the Closed Lost list?
- When can SDRs use the names of existing clients in their outbounding efforts?

Those are just a few samples of situations that require written rules of engagement to be in place. No two companies are the same. I'm sure you can think of a few more situations to add to the list. You may as well get them all written down in a document or in your SDR playbook and have SDRs sign off on it.

BARGAINING

When the rules are unclear or if the existing policy is not fair, you will want to negotiate a fair outcome with your SDRs.

To give you an example, "Dale", one of my top-performing SDRs, called into an account that belonged to "Chip," one of my poorest-performing SDRs. When Dale posted on our team Slack channel that he had booked a meeting with this company, guess who Slacks me five minutes later? You guessed it. Chip.

When I looked at the account history in our CRM, it was evident that Chip hadn't put much effort into booking a meeting with prospects on this account. There was a call here. An email there. No more than two touches per contact.

Chip had never had a conversation with anyone at the company. And no one bothered to respond to his one-email strategy.

Dale, on the other hand, called four different contacts three times, sent them LinkedIn connection requests, and sent all of them three emails. When one of the prospects finally picked up the phone, Dale used his skills to book the meeting.

But the written rules of engagement said that if the lead was touched within 30 days and another SDR booked a meeting with them, the original account owning SDR would get the credit for the meeting.

What a dilemma. Clearly Chip found a loophole in our rules of engagement and wanted to take full credit (and commission) for Dale's hard work.

After some careful thinking, I decided to compromise. Written rules are written rules. So I begrudgingly gave Chip the credit for booking the qualified meeting. Naturally, Dale was fuming. So I made him a deal.

Instead of giving Dale credit for the meeting he booked, I gave him quota relief. The Outbound SDRs had a goal for 10 qualified meetings per month. I temporarily lowered Dale's to nine. That allowed him to hit 111% of quota for the month.

Chip got his credit, yet he still only hit 10% of his goal.

Soon after, Dale was promoted, and Chip was put on a PIP.

The moral to this story is that not all the written rules will make sense for every situation. It's important that you are prepared to think on your feet and pivot when that time comes.

OTHER REFEREE SITUATIONS

As an SDR leader, you will be called upon to help settle other disputes involving the people you lead.

Sometimes SDRs have a personality clash with the AEs they work with. You may have to facilitate a meeting to get to the bottom of the dispute. If the dispute cannot be resolved, you may need to reassign the SDR to another AE.

Perhaps an SDR on your team mistakenly calls on an account an AE is already near closing. Put on your referee hat.

Most Customer Success reps hate it when SDRs call on their existing client accounts by accident. It's bound to happen. CRMs have duplicate records. Companies change names. Companies get acquired or merge with others.

When a Customer Success Rep is breathing down your SDR's neck for calling their account, it will be up to you to be the ref and settle the dispute.

Are you missing being an individual contributor right about now?

Remember when you only had to be accountable for yourself?

Well, welcome to leadership, my friend.

Don't get me wrong. Leading SDRs is a rewarding experience.

You get to amplify yourself and watch your team become mini-yous. You are able to influence the next generation of sales professionals and sales leaders. Executive leaders give you kudos and publicly recognize you.

And you get to make more money than you ever could as an SDR. You might also get promoted and earn even more money.

But you will *earn* that extra cheddar when settling disputes within your SDR organization, disputes between SDRs and AEs, and disputes between SDRs and Customer Success Reps.

In fact, it's almost like you need a degree in psychology to be successful in this role.

You may as well do like I did and get yourself a subscription to *Psychology Today* because the subject matter in the next chapter will surely make the magazine come in handy.

Chapter 14

PSYCHOLOGIST

Many of the people you see every day are fighting personal battles you know nothing about. This includes the people you lead. So, when an SDR comes to you with a problem they are facing at work or outside of work, consider it a compliment. It means you've earned their trust.

More companies are placing an emphasis on employees' mental health. They are offering free access to apps like Headspace and Calm. They are making sure their health insurance covers mental wellness. And they are giving employees enough time off to deal with their mental health issues without them having to worry about losing their jobs.

I know you didn't sign up to be a psychologist, but it doesn't hurt to listen to the reps you lead when they share their personal problems. You might discover an underlying condition about why their work is suffering. You may find an opportunity to establish stronger bonds with them. You might even be able to prevent a tragedy.

You don't need to move a comfy couch into your office. No need to ask, "And how did that make you *feel*?" Just listen.

You may be taken aback by some of the things the SDRs on your team share with you. Whatever they share, treat it like they have doctor/patient confidentiality.

Here are some situations SDRs have shared with me that I was able to help them with:
- An SDR's close family member contracted Covid-19.
- A rep was moonlighting for Uber at night to help make ends meet.
- An SDR was on the verge of becoming homeless.
- A rep's best friend was murdered.
- An ex was stalking an SDR's spouse.
- An SDR's roommate stole her ATM card and withdrew $500.
- A rep's friend committed suicide.
- An SDR was living in a car.
- A rep's spouse was ending their marriage.
- An SDR's car was repossessed.
- A rep's family member texted in sick for them while the rep was in jail.
- An SDR got his girlfriend pregnant, and his wife found out.

That's just a sample of the situations I've dealt with while leading SDR teams. Each situation was different. Some situations were downright shocking. Yet I was able to maintain my composure, listen to what the SDRs had to say, and even express empathy when it was appropriate.

Keep in mind that it is not your job to solve your reps' personal problems. Allowing them to vocalize the issue may be enough for them to solve the problems on their own.

Always keep in mind that the people you lead are struggling with demons you know nothing about. And sometimes they'll trust you enough to share them with you. Be prepared to listen and to empathize.

If you uncover a situation that's a threat to the SDR's health and well-being, delegate helping to HR. Allow HR to provide referrals to the professional resources they may need.

Ultimately, your job is to inspire your team, motivate your team, and coach them to generate meetings and pipeline. But even when you're doing your best, SDRs are bound to leave your team because of promotions, terminations, or just from them finding a company that is a better fit.

That's why it's important to always be on the lookout for new talent to join your team. You'll need to put on your recruiter hat for that. For some tips and ideas on how to attract top talent, turn to the next chapter.

Chapter 15

RECRUITER

Given the short-term nature of the modern SDR role, you need to always be on the lookout for talented SDRs. One of the best ways to ensure you have that talent is through personally recruiting top candidates.

Recruiting SDRs can be tricky. In most organizations, the SDR role is considered an entry-level role. Some companies require a couple of years of sales experience. There are even career SDR roles that require several years of experience.

Not every SDR role is the same. You have Inbound, Outbound, SMB, Mid-Market, Enterprise, Chat SDRs, Research SDRs, Government, Commercial, SaaS, and non-tech SDRs.

To be successful at recruiting, you must know what good looks like. Since we can't just clone our top performers, we must decide what behavior traits to look for within SDRs.

BEHAVIOR TRAITS AND SKILLS

Depending on who you ask, there are at least 10 common traits that hiring managers look for within BDRs. Among them are:

Resiliency - SDRs need to understand that part of the role is dealing with rejection and objections. Not everyone needs what you sell. Some people won't have the time to listen to what you have to say. Many people will object to having their day interrupted. Some people won't have the power to make buying decisions. Others won't have the budget. Some prospects will already have what you sell. Other people are opposed to change.

SDRs not only need to anticipate rejection and objections but they have to quickly get over it all. If they dwell on the rejection and allow fear and self-doubt to creep in, it will affect their ability to be successful in the role.

SDR Managers can gauge resiliency by asking candidates to name a challenge they have faced and how they overcame it.

Coachability - SDRs need to be able to take the information you teach them and run with it. If they are stuck in their ways, have mental blockers, or simply can't adapt, it can be impossible to coach them.

SDR Managers can test for coachability by doing cold call role plays. Provide a script to candidates. Role play with them for the first time. Then give them two or three tips on how to improve. Then ask them to go through role play again and to implement the coaching you gave them. If the second role play sounds like the first one, the candidate is probably not coachable.

This is why the coaching framework I mentioned earlier is vital. After coaching SDRs in one coaching session, ask them to demonstrate what they learned in the beginning of your next session before continuing to a new subject. If SDRs cannot repeatedly demonstrate what they have learned, it lets you know they are not coachable.

This lack of coachability will show up in their work. When you listen to their recorded calls or read their emails to prospects and see they haven't leveraged your coaching, it will hurt them and you.

Optimism - Successful SDRs look forward to the future. They expect their outcomes to improve. They look forward to their company's changes and growth. They expect to get better at their jobs, to get promoted, and to earn more money. They can be a positive influence amongst the team.

A pessimistic SDR, on the other hand, may have a "Woe is me," attitude. They see the glass as half empty. They think their careers can't get better. They don't believe in the company.

Optimism is a little tougher to gauge in the interview process. You may have to use psychometric testing to better understand SDRs' optimism.

Otherwise, simply asking candidates what they are looking forward to may help you to understand if the candidate is optimistic or pessimistic.

Organizational Skills - SDRs need to be able to organize their days, their calendars, and the tasks within their software. That means knowing how to prioritize what's important, using time blocks to perform specific tasks (like call blocks), and keeping up with due tasks on their calendars, in their CRM, and in their sales enablement platforms.

Process-Orientation - Plain and simple: SDRs need the skills to be able to follow a process. Examples include all the steps to take after booking a qualified meeting like updating the CRM, sending invitations to prospects and AEs, and taking prospects out of cadences.

Competitiveness - One way to ensure you are recruiting A-Players is to search for candidates who have a need to win. A need to be number one. A need to be recognized.

Competitive SDRs will study the top SDRs within your organization. They may even ask for their help and mentorship.

SDRs who are competitive will also put in the extra work. They will dedicate more time to learning about what you sell, learning about buyer personas, and learning how to overcome objections.

Competitive SDRs will also be incredibly efficient within their 40-hour workweek. Or they will put in time beyond the 40 hours.

When I was an SDR, I spent two to four hours every Saturday morning researching new prospects to contact and adding them to my CRM.

And if I went through a full day without booking a meeting, I'd put in a couple of hours overtime to try reaching prospects outside of my time zone.

Ambition - The SDRs who expect promotions and growth tend to do whatever it takes to get it done. That starts with being successful as an SDR. While some may only want to attain the highest-level SDR position (and the money that comes with it), others will want to become AEs or managers.

During the interview process, it is important to ask candidates what they want their careers to look like after the SDR role. If they can't see beyond the SDR role, they may become stagnant SDRs.

If you rely upon SDRs to be a bench for the AE role, it's important to ascertain that SDRs want a closing role next.

Ambitious SDRs will be money motivated. Ask them why they want to be AEs or managers. Chances are, it will be because of the money they can earn.

Curiosity - Continuous learners make great SDRs. They ask questions, find great resources, and dedicate their time to learning. Expect them to ask you a lot of questions, especially when they first start. Expect them to ask AEs, marketing, and other SDRs lots of questions too.

Curious SDRs will want to know more about the products and services you sell. They'll expect to understand the entire sales process from research and cold outreach to running demos and closing deals.

SDRs who are curious will leverage books, webinars, blogs, events, and online courses to satisfy their thirst for knowledge. They'll utilize internal resources like your learning management system, intranet, and Slack channel to learn.

To uncover curiosity during the interview process, ask candidates about the last thing they went to learn about on their own and the resources they used to learn it. Most will tell you how they read a book, attended a class, or watched a YouTube video.

Speaking Voice - Because SDRs speak with lots of prospects and admins over the phone, it's important that they have great-sounding voices. That includes leaving voicemails. Their voices need to sound professional. They should sound enthused. And they should use proper pronunciation.

Writing Skills - SDRs will use the written word to communicate with prospects. This includes through email, social media, direct mail, online chat, and even texts. Outside of phone calls and personalized video, all other communication with prospects is through the written word.

Poorly written communication to your prospects can be embarrassing and unprofessional. It makes SDRs look bad. It makes you look bad as a coach. It makes the company look bad too.

During the interview process, give candidates a writing prompt. Ask them to send a mock email to you as if you are a prospect.

OTHER TRAITS AND SKILLS

Confidence and enthusiasm are a must. I'm sure you can think of other traits and skills SDR candidates must possess to be successful. Perhaps you've recognized these traits and skills within your top performing SDRs. Be sure to take the time to write them down.

Remind your internal recruiters to be on the lookout for those traits and skills. Write out your own interview questions to look for those traits and skills.

WHERE TO FIND SDR CANDIDATES

Internal Referrals

Chances are, your top SDRs (and AEs) know other top SDRs. Maybe they worked together at another company. Perhaps they belong to the same social media groups. They may have even met at a trade show.

However, not all employees are motivated by helping simply for the good of the team. That's why an employee referral bonus program is a must. Remember, SDRs are money motivated. When you pay them to find strong candidates, they'll put in the effort to contact the people they know to be a good fit.

Let's keep in mind that competitive SDRs might not always refer the very best candidates if they feel they will outshine them. No one wants new hires to make them look bad, especially if they referred them.

Outsourced Business Development Firms

Having worked for a couple of outsourced business development firms, I can attest that they produce some excellent SDRs. That's because those SDRs prospect on behalf of many different companies in many different industries. That means that they speak to lots of different personas and tons of gatekeepers.

Another reason you want to recruit SDRs within those organizations is because they are notoriously underpaid. You can pay them more, and they will be motivated to come work for you.

Also, SDRs at third-party firms are overworked. They manage two to six projects at a time. When I worked for them, I was prospecting on behalf of at least three different companies a week. Working directly for the firm they are outbounding for instead will be a welcomed change.

When I first started working for these types of companies, there were no more than 20 well-known ones. Now there are hundreds if not thousands of outsourced business development firms. A different one seems to pitch me every week.

SDR Bootcamps

SDR bootcamps are good at finding non-traditional candidates (those without four-year degrees or tech sales experience) and training them to become SDRs.

They expose them to the most up-to-date software, like sales enablement platforms, CRMs, and research databases.

They teach them outbounding skills like how to get past gatekeepers, how to overcome objections, and how to ask for meetings.

No two bootcamps are the same.

Some focus more on email outbounding skills than cold calling skills.

Some charge students to attend the bootcamps.

Some charge employers to place bootcamp graduates.

I have personally hired a handful of bootcamp graduates, and they have not disappointed. Some have even had an advantage over more traditional candidates with four-year degrees.

Other Firms

While many companies still see the SDR role as more of an entry-level role than a career, there are still opportunities to hire experienced SDRs. You'll find them working for other tech firms or even working for non-tech firms. I spent two and a half years working as an SDR for a logistics firm.

To find these candidates, you will need to use more traditional means, like LinkedIn.

On LinkedIn, especially if you are using their paid services, you can run queries based on the criteria you require.

Reach out to these people. Direct message them. Email them. Call them if you must. Get them excited about the idea of working for you and working for your company. Doing this will distinguish you from other hiring managers who mostly rely on recruiters to do this for them.

When reaching out to these candidates, you'll naturally want to accentuate the things that make your company a place they will want to work. Better pay, benefits, unlimited time off, great career path, and even the ability to be fully remote are just a few things you could amplify.

Job Posting

You may be called upon to write a job description that will appear on job boards. The boards could be on sites like LinkedIn, Indeed, Glassdoor, ZipRecruiter, and Monster.

This is especially true if you are building an SDR team from scratch.

Don't feel pressured to reinvent the wheel. Instead, take a look at job postings for SDR positions at other companies. Take the best of them all. Add your own flavor and highlight what makes working for your company unique.

Work with HR

If your organization is large enough, there is a good chance you have an HR team complete with internal recruiters. Work with them to let them know what you are looking for in an SDR candidate. Help them to determine how best to screen candidates so that your time is not wasted interviewing people who will not be a fit.

External Recruiters

If the budget is available, you may decide to hire a recruiting agency to find your ideal SDR candidates. While this isn't always the most cost-effective way to find entry-level to mid-level employees, it may be a time-saver. Just make sure to outsource this function to a firm with a strong reputation and experience in hiring SDRs as opposed to full-cycle sales reps. While SDRs and full-cycle reps have similar skill sets, they are still very different roles.

Speaking of outsourcing, there may come a time when you decide to outsource the SDR job to a firm. Before determining if a third-party firm is right for you, you should definitely read the next chapter.

Chapter 16

THE OUTSOURCER

In your role as an SDR leader, you may be given the opportunity to outsource some of your business development to a third-party organization. Having worked for three such organizations and having hired and/or managed the relationship with four of them, I have a few opinions about them.

Many growing sales teams get to the point when they have to decide if they should hire employees to do sales development work or hire third-party vendors. They want to know the best options for booking meetings, reducing SDR turnover, and maximizing productivity while keeping costs down. Should they outsource? Should they keep the SDR function in place? Or maybe they should try a blended approach.

Let's start with costs…

COSTS

Based on The Bridge Group's 2021 Metrics and Compensation Report for Sales Development, the average SDR is paid $76,000 OTE. Add an average of $10,000 a year for healthcare benefits, and we're looking at $86,000 per SDR. When your SDRs are handing off multiple prospects that develop into buying customers, the closed deals cover the reps' salaries and then some.

Calculating the cost of third-party reps can be a bit trickier because outsourced teleprospecting firms tend to charge different rates. Some charge up-front costs for items like call script development, prospect lists, and kickoff meetings. That can cost you a one-time fee anywhere between $5000 to $20,000.

Then there is the cost of the actual outbounding, which can cost from $60 an hour to $250 an hour. If you hire a third-party firm for a full year at the low end of the spectrum, you're looking at $124,800 just for the labor.

The good thing about outsourced firms is that you're not married to them if you hire them. If you have a short-term project, for example, you may only need to work with them for three months instead of for years on end. Plus, you don't have to pay their reps' health benefits or unemployment benefits once the gig is over.

Recently, I managed the relationship with an outsourced business development firm I inherited. While they generated some pipeline, it was not the amount of pipeline they forecasted. After a six-month relationship, their contract ended. We did not renew it.

I've had similar results with other firms. They over-promised and under-delivered. And the relationship was short term.

There was one exception. I managed the relationship with an excellent third-party firm out of the United Kingdom. They taught our internal SDR team a thing or two on how to book qualified meetings with prospects. They had already worked two years with a software firm I joined prior to my arrival. After a year with the firm, they were still in place after I had moved on.

SKILLS

It's the luck of the draw when it comes to hiring an outsourced firm to prospect for your company. You might get the person straight out of college with no experience assigned to your project; or you might get the rep who has been prospecting for three years (a lifetime in this world).

The good thing about third-party firms is that they tend to work with a lot of different companies in a lot of different verticals giving their reps lots of experience. Chances are, their reps have already worked in your vertical by the time you decide to hire them. So, even if it's at the surface level, the more experienced reps can at least talk the talk if they get in the weeds with a challenging prospect.

Nowadays, the average SDRs are staying on their team between a year to 18 months before moving up or moving out. This results in them getting less experience. When I worked for these types of firms, they relied heavily on call scripts and email scripts written by someone other than the reps doing the calling and emailing.

On the other hand, internal SDRs end up with a deeper knowledge of the company's products and services. Onboarding tends to be more thorough. And internal resources like sales managers, field sales reps, and even marketing teams are usually willing to help an employee succeed much more than they are a rep from an outsourced firm.

In fact, when I worked for third-party firms, I found many of the clients' AEs to be combative. I wouldn't even think of asking them for help with product understanding, common lingo, or objection handling when I was at an outsourced firm. When working as an internal SDR, I could take conversations with prospects way beyond the surface level, which included smart objection-handling, actively participating in discovery calls, running discovery calls on my own, and showing demos by myself.

THE X-FACTOR

When I think of the colleagues I worked with and the reps I trained while working on SDR teams as an employee, I'm reminded that it wasn't always a wonderful experience.

Many SDRs lacked the motivation to be the best they could be. Some were just biding their time until they could move on to become customer success managers, AEs, or marketers. Others dreamed of doing something else with their lives.

And some just didn't want to put in the work to be great at the job. They didn't read books. Didn't attend webinars on their own. Thought role-play was a waste of time. Didn't even care if they ranked 8th in performance out of 10 reps.

Third-party firms had SDRs who were more competitive with each other. Contests meant something, not just for the prizes of monetary value but also for the right to be called the best.

Even if the SDRs didn't love it, ongoing training was a staple at these firms. There was role play, teaching objection-handling, training at weekly meetings, and a sharing of resources like books and webinars.

Though those things did occur at these companies, it didn't make up for the downside of working there. High turnover, representing four to six different companies a week, and checking your brain at the door were common practice.

Call metrics were between 80-100 dials a day without an auto-dialer. The reps were underpaid. While the company might have been making $124,000 a year on their labor, best believe the average SDR was making only a third of that.

And because they quit more often, the clients got to go through the crapshoot process three or four times a year, hoping to get paired up with a rep who could produce.

To top it all off, if clients decided they wanted to hire high-producing SDRs away from these firms, the non-solicitation agreements within the contracts would not allow it. Some firms have gotten smarter about that by just requiring their clients to pay a fee to permanently hire their reps. They act sort of like a headhunter.

Because I had deeper product knowledge, the pay was better pay, I received inbound leads (which never happens at third-party firms), and I didn't have to worry about focusing on six different value props a week. I liked being an internal SDR more than working for outsourced firms.

Before you consider hiring a third-party firm, take costs, skills, and forecasted pipeline into consideration.

By the way, you can also outsource account and contact research. You can find inexpensive specialists on websites like fiverr and Upwork. Less research for your team means more time for outbounding.

Is your head spinning from learning about all the hats you must wear to be an effective SDR Manager? Tell your boss you deserve a SPIFF.

One of the best things about leading an internal team is that you get to help craft their rewards and SPIFFs. If you need some ideas on how to reward your team, turn to the next section.

Part 3

REWARDING SDRS

Chapter 17

MONEY

When I first got started in sales, money was my primary motivation. I imagined using those huge commission checks to pay for lavish vacations, luxury cars, and my kids' college education. For many SDRs, the amount of money they make is their primary motivation. Employers know this, which is why many of them place no limit on the amount of money a salesperson can earn in commissions and bonuses. The more you sell, the more you earn.

As a hiring manager, you know that total compensation is a huge motivator for salespeople. Yet many of you are guarded when it comes to sharing this information up front. Why not at least provide the salary range in your ads or even during the first interview?

I learned to get the "money thing" out of the way a long time ago. But I had to learn the hard way. I'd applied for a position I'd found through a classified ad. I submitted my resume even though the ad mentioned nothing about the pay range. I figured the potential employer would simply look at my experience and education and know what type of compensation I'd be expecting. That was my first mistake.

The company invited me in for an interview. When I arrived, they asked me to complete a paper application. I did as requested. When it came to salary history, I did what I always do. I wrote "will discuss." I had always been taught that the first one to give a number loses.

After the interview, it was determined that I could be a good fit. So the human resources manager scheduled a second interview with the company's owner. Neither of us discussed salary. That was my second mistake.

The second interview went just as well. The owner liked me just as much as the HR manager. After that interview, I figured he would send me an offer letter. He didn't. And I didn't ask about money during the interview. Third mistake.

Instead of an offer letter, I received a phone call asking me to return for the third interview. Instead of being cautious, I was excited. This was it! They were bringing me in to make me an offer, and I wouldn't have to bring up money first.

After the group interview, the owner made me an offer. Minimum wage. I was hurt. I was angry. I was flabbergasted. Three interviews. Three excuses for leaving my current job for an hour or so each day. All for a minimum wage offer.

With such a low offer, I imagined that company had a high turnover. And if turnover is high, best believe it affects the morale of the rest of the sales staff. Who wants to be a part of a company with a revolving door?

I bring up this personal story for a few reasons. First of all, being transparent about your salary creates a huge advantage for the employer. They won't waste employees' time on advertising to them and interviewing candidates who will never work for them.

Secondly, getting the basic compensation discussion out of the way allows more time to discover if the candidate is a true fit.

And finally, candidates need to learn to prevent situations like this from ever happening.

I eliminated this problem by simply stating my salary history on my resume. After all, no employer in his right mind would call on a candidate and ask them to work for them for less money than they are already making.

The structure of salary and commission can make a huge difference too. Many superstars prefer to earn 100% commission. Some account managers who may have the responsibility of upselling or calling into existing accounts might fall on the other end of the spectrum. Those folks prefer a higher salary and less dependency on a commission check. Most of us fall somewhere in the middle.

One potential employer asked me why I preferred to earn a base salary instead of 100% commission. I told him that it served as a safety net for the things I was unable to control, like a down economy, a product or service that has become irrelevant to sell, or market saturation.

When creating your compensation structure, you need to be acutely aware of how salespeople behave when it comes to selling. We tend to focus on the things that pay us best.

For many salespeople, salary and commission is the number one motivator for staying in sales. Surprisingly, it's not the number one motivator for all of them.

INSTANT GRATIFICATION

Instant gratification rewards serve as great motivators. Gift cards, company outings, luncheons, and even time off can spark positive activities from SDRs who want to be rewarded for their work. For example, the team with the most pipeline for the month could all be rewarded with $100 gift cards for a steakhouse. Or the individual who meets with the most prospects in a week could be rewarded a paid day off.

These types of rewards help employees to stay focused on shorter-term company goals. Like I said before, employees will focus on the things that pay them well. So, if there is a specific behavior you would like to encourage, find a way to reward employees for accomplishing these goals.

Do you need some reward ideas? Try these:
- $100 movie theater gift cards.
- A paid Friday off.
- Two tickets to a professional sports game.
- Office space for a week.
- A luxury rental car for a month.
- Dinner for four.
- Bowling, food, and drinks for the team.

When rewarding the individual or team for a job well done, don't just drop the gifts at their desks. Instead, give them their rewards in front of the entire team. Let everyone else know what they can earn for a job well done. Allow high performers to bask in the glory. Though a round of applause might not be big, it sure is better than keeping rewards a big secret.

When I polled the SDRs on teams I have led, the first thing I asked them was how they like to be rewarded for a job well done. The next chapter provides one of the most common answers.

Chapter 18

RECOGNITION

Let's face it; most companies are horrible at publicly recognizing their sales staff. The folks who are opposed to it are usually the curmudgeons who believe their employees' paychecks should be motivating enough.

They're not.

What if your sales leaders took a mere two extra minutes to shout out the best performers of the week? What if the best SDRs received a framed certificate for having the most meetings in a month? Sometimes a plaque is all they want.

What if they were rewarded with a banquet attended by other high-ranking executives in the company?

Sure, those attaboy emails are fine. They're just not extraordinary. It reminds me of a personal story.

During the Great Recession of 2008, our company president and vice president of sales at a 3PL summoned me to the president's office. Being that I had a one-hour commute, I wasn't always the most on-time employee. That coupled with the down economy, I thought I was being let go.

Turns out, the bosses thought I was doing a fantastic job in the sales department. In fact, they thought I was doing such a great job that they asked me if I would train seven non-sales employees to do what I did. Training them would help the company stay afloat, and it would save those seven employees' jobs.

Feeling grateful that I wasn't about to get canned, I gladly took on the challenge. I rolled up my sleeves and got to work. I created training materials, which included a slide deck and cheat sheets. After the training, I supervised the newly formed SDR staff until they could function on their own.

The project was a huge success. While similar companies were going out of business, we remained profitable, and nobody lost their jobs.

When it came time to reward me for leading and executing this project, I was presented with a $50 gift card and a company sweatshirt.

That's all.

Not exactly fireworks. This was the strike of a match and the sound of a kazoo.

Did it motivate me? Absolutely! I updated my resume that night.

The moral of this story is to do your best to match rewards with efforts. I thought I should have received a promotion, a raise, and my own staff to permanently supervise.

If Jim brings in an additional $100,000 a month in pipeline, don't just send an attaboy email. If Susan surpasses all company Closed Won goals, don't just give her a plaque. Give her a reward that surpasses all other rewards. Not only will it motivate Susan to keep bringing it but it will also motivate the other salespeople to bring it too.

Need some ideas on how to publicly motivate your SDR team? Try these:

- Send attaboy emails.
- Forward kudos emails from customers.
- Give gift cards at the weekly sales meeting.
- Have a special lunch delivered to the SDR's desk.
- Take the team out for an awards banquet.
- Give keys to a rented luxury car to the top performer at the annual company meeting.
- Pay employees cash when they "ring the bell" after booking a meeting.
- Post pictures of the company trip for all to see when it is earned as a result of being a top performer.
- Rent a football field, hire cheerleaders, and shoot fireworks in honor of the top performer.

The next chapter explains how you can invest in your reps for the long term.

Chapter 19

EDUCATION

It's obvious that companies benefit from having smart employees. That's why many employers have education requirements, such as a high school diploma, a bachelor's degree, or even a doctorate.

What's not so obvious is why employers don't continue to invest in their employees' education. When you think about it, things change all the time. This includes the world of sales.

How has selling changed over the years? There are all kinds of methodologies like Selling Through Curiosity, The Challenger Sales model, and Sandler Training.

Then there have been changes in technology like web conferencing, video conferencing, smartphones, social media, and e-commerce. Even collegiate education has changed by offering bachelor's degrees and master's degrees in sales. When I was in college, the closest you could get to a degree in sales was a marketing degree.

A huge way to motivate your SDRs is to pay for their college education. If a high school graduate wants to get a bachelor's, why not help them pay for it? If an SDR has a bachelor's degree but wants to pursue one of those master's degrees in sales, why not reimburse them for it?

Education reimbursement is another fantastic way to attract and retain good SDRs. It's also a way to ensure you keep quality employees with relevant knowledge to help your company. Take a page from the United States military's playbook for this one.

Even if you're a small business with a limited budget, you can still contribute to your SDR team's continuous education. If money is tight, only reimburse the employees when they get a B or an A. Or agree to pay for half of the employee's tuition. You could even pay for something less expensive like their books. The important thing is to be a contributor if you want to motivate your employees.

When speaking of education, it doesn't have to be formal college coursework. There are also continuing education courses and seminars. How about paying for webinar registration fees? Or how about reimbursing any sales or marketing book purchases? After all, your SDRs are learning more to sell more and to ultimately make you more money.

There was a popular meme on social media that posed a hypothetical question. One person asks, "What if we pay for our employees' education and they leave?" The other replies, "What if we don't and they stay?"

Another question to ask is this: "What if we don't pay for our employees' education and things change within the industry such as how people buy?"

Also: "What if our competitor pays for their employees' education?" I pose these questions because many employers simply accept the status quo. But accepting the status quo is a surefire way to become irrelevant.

If you want to motivate your sales team, ask your company to invest in your team's education. And when they graduate, celebrate!

But don't just invest in continuous education. Require it. You don't have to make all of your SDR team go back to college. But it would make sense to encourage an ongoing learning environment.

At one company I worked for, all employees were given access to free Udemy courses.

At another company, the employees were given free access to LinkedIn Learning courses.

I curated courses that would help the SDRs on my team to get better at their jobs like professional email writing, account-based marketing courses, and inbound sales.

I also encouraged them to take courses that would help them in life, like a seven-hour personal finance class and a quick course on how to overcome fear.

Maintaining a continuous education environment can be achieved by appointing team leaders as mentors, using sales meeting times to role play, and allowing employees to attend business-related webinars on company time.

Encourage SDRs to take advantage of free access to courses when they are offered. Make them aware of other resources like HubSpot Academy, edX, Coursera, Pluralsight, Udemy, and BrightTALK that offer free or inexpensive courses.

Not every company has the budget to pay for their employees' college education. But surely, they could pay a registration fee or reimburse the cost of a book. Right?

If you want to motivate your SDR team, ask your executive leadership to invest in their continuous education for their personal growth and your company's growth.

As they say, work hard, play harder. The next chapter explains how you can give SDRs something to look forward to.

Chapter 20

FUN

In my life before Sales, I worked on the other side of the phone. I was a buyer for a stuffy, Fortune 500 office supply company. The money was decent. The environment was professional with plenty of room to grow. The problem was, they didn't know how to have fun.

A fun work environment is a primary motivator for new SDRs (especially millennials and Generation Z) to stay on with a company.

When it comes to fun, management needs to think beyond the boring old annual company picnic. Nowadays, companies attract and retain great salespeople by providing ping pong tables, foosball tables, pool tables, and video gaming systems. (Board games like Scrabble and chess work for older people like me.)

They also know how to have fun by getting out of the building. Bowling, ice-skating, whirly-ball, golfing, skiing, paintball, and professional sports outings are just a sample of the events companies are encouraging employees to take part in. Not only are they fun events but they also serve as team building exercises. (But do you really need an excuse to have fun?)

You can even incorporate fun within your daily sales activities. There are several gamification companies like Ambition that provide leaderboards, sports-themed scoreboards, and rewards systems for individual salespeople and SDR teams. (How cool would it be to post their stats the way the sports teams do?) If you don't want to invest in any formal gamification tools, a simple yet fun contest could do the trick.

Need ideas on how to have a fun work environment? Here are a few ideas:
- Shut down the office half a day and have the office attend a major league baseball game.
- Play Twister at lunch time.
- Organize a virtual escape room event
- Have a Fortnite tournament.
- Hire a comedian to perform during lunch.
- Let a winning team go bowling on your tab.
- Make a losing team clean the kitchen.
- Have a bring-your-dog-to-work day.
- Have a company movie night.
- Hand out Dave & Buster's game cards.
- Karaoke
- Have a dance battle.
- Play *Cards Against Humanity* together

When it comes to encouraging fun with co-workers in and out of the office, the sky's the limit. And remember happy employees tend to be loyal employees.

They say employees want to be part of something greater than themselves. The next chapter is a great way to help SDRs do just that.

Chapter 21

INTRAPRENUERS

Imagine if your company had a business inside of your business. And what if that business turned out to not only help you to better compete against competitors but also helped you to grow profits? What if you had a current employee with the intelligence to run their own company but would prefer to be an intrapreneur (business owner inside of another business)? Imagine the kind of motivation that would be for your smart employee.

Intrapreneur programs are one of the latest and greatest ways to keep employees motivated beyond your wildest dreams. They let employees know that you value their work. They in turn become loyal employees. The kicker is that instead of going out on their own, taking some of your customers with them, and becoming a competitor, they help your business instead.

If intrapreneurship is such a good idea, why are so many business owners against them? For starters, they feel threatened if an employee is as intelligent or even more intelligent than they are. They feel like they might have to relinquish some power to work with the intrapreneur. Some also feel that there is nothing stopping the intrapreneur from developing a product or service within their current company and then going out on their own anyway. Of course, there are legal precautions business owners can take to prevent the latter. But the amount of time and work it takes to prepare themselves legally can also be a deterrent.

Still, if you want to motivate your team without having to compete against them later down the road, intrapreneurship is a great way to go. Perhaps it's time for you to move beyond the feedback form and move into a more meaningful program.

Another way to motivate SDRs is by giving them more (or at least different) responsibilities. Coupled with a new title, they could serve as a great motivator.

Why would an SDR take on more responsibilities and a new title without being compensated for it?

Several reasons, including gaining practical business experience. For those who want to advance their careers, for example, a team leader position might serve as a motivator. They know that the experience can help them grow within the company and later in their careers.

It might also help them if they even decide to become entrepreneurs. In fact, there are several entrepreneurs today who got their start by learning everything they could about how their previous employers ran the company. They become jacks of all trades by learning accounting, sales, marketing, management, and more.

In some cultures, the new title is even more important than the pay increase. In other words, they'd rather be a team leader making $70,000 a year than an SDR making $100,000 a year.

You will find that as an SDR's career develops, money is important but it's not everything. Autonomy, better titles, and a chance to lead are just as rewarding.

And let's not forget freedom.

The next chapter explains how you can add more freedom into the lives of the SDRs on your team.

Chapter 22

REMOTE

The Covid-19 pandemic surely proved remote work is a viable option. Remember when I told you about that boss who rewarded my efforts with helping to save the company by presenting me with a $50 gift card and a company sweatshirt? My work with that company is also a great source for a story about remote work.

Back in 2008, I took an SDR position that was an hour's commute from home. For some, the commute is no big deal. But for those who live in areas where winters are brutal, the commute can be a dealbreaker.

After I had proven myself to be a great and trustworthy SDR and then a leader and trainer who helped save the company, I requested the opportunity to work from home. After all, I only needed a telephone and a computer with Internet services to do my job. The sweatshirt presenters denied me yet again.

What were they thinking? Even back then we had webcams, web conference software, call tracking software, and a CRM. Why wouldn't they allow one of their top performers to work from home? That was the straw that broke the camel's back.

Working from home for me would have provided an escape from the daily, white-knuckled commute, a tremendous savings in fuel costs, and the ability to focus like never before instead of dealing with the distractions of office politics and unnecessary social interactions, like water cooler gossip.

Not only did I leave that company, I left the state and moved south. Heck, if I was ever asked to commute again, at least it wouldn't be on black ice and snow.

When I think back to the times I've worked from home before the pandemic, I recollect that I did more work and was more productive. I stuffed envelopes with sales letters while watching TV at night. I worked through lunch while researching information on prospects. And I was way less stressed before making my first sales call of the day.

Before dismissing the idea of allowing SDRs on your team permanently working remote, consider the benefits.

The company will spend less money on utilities, office space, and coffee.

Most top performers use the commute time they gain back to put in more hours, which results in more pipeline. And working from home can be a strong loyalty builder for your team.

Of course, if performance wanes, you can still have SDRs come back to work in the office.

Allowing your team to work remotely will not only save you money but it will also build loyalty within your sales team.

What's surprising is how so many sales leaders are pushing a return to the office. Though it's encouraging that they are being creative by offering half days off on Fridays. Some are exploring the hybrid model as well, where SDRs work remote two days a week.

OFFICE SPACE

When it comes to sales, I believe cubicles are the worst invention ever! They're loud. They're small. They give the illusion of privacy even though they provide very little. And customers and prospects get that call center vibe they hear other SDRs speaking in the background.

Open space environments (cubicles without walls) are no better.

But business owners must maximize office space and keep costs down. Therefore, tight working environments are a necessary evil. But if business owners and managers want to motivate their top performers, providing office space is one way to go. There are several ways you can provide office space for SDRs. They include:

1. Providing good old-fashioned phone rooms for distraction-free conversations.

2. Allowing top performers to "win" office space for their achievements. This could be achieved through short-term or long-term contests. The top SDRs get office space for a month or even a year. If an SDR without an office outperforms an SDR with one, they get the office. What a way to motivate high performance!
3. Valuing employees more than game rooms. (Yes, put the ping pong table in an open space and give that space to a top performer.)

Employers also need to give up on the notion that poor performers are going to learn to be top performers simply by sitting next to them. That strategy hardly ever works because many SDRs prefer to use their own style of selling, even if it's unsuccessful.

Instead of hoping for optimization through osmosis, managers must take the responsibility of mentoring SDRs for success. They can do so by providing great on-the-job training, education programs, and role-playing sessions.

Does it make sense to punish a top performer by removing them from their office into the cubicles or open spaces because of the belief of optimization through osmosis? Of course not. But it happens.

It happened to me. I was rewarded for my great performance. Then management assumed that if only the new reps could hear me live, they would become top performers as well. So instead of enjoying the reward for my hard work, I was relocated back to the noisy, distracting, tight space with

SDRs on either side of me. The people sitting next to me heard me succeed yet continued the status quo.

If tight spaces are a must, business owners should choose spaces with high ceilings. Smaller offices allow noise to bounce off the walls thus creating a noisier office. An ideal call center would be a warehouse where the ceilings are high. So even while sitting in side-by-side spaces, it will be more difficult for employees to disturb each other.

Ask executive leadership to provide the proper spacing between desks so that noise and distraction are not factors in the SDR team's overall success or failure.

Want to motivate your SDR team? Give them space to do their job.

The next chapter goes into how you can give SDRs even more freedom than what office space or working remotely can provide. Because sometimes, they just need to get away from it all.

Chapter 23

VACATIONS

I wanted a pay increase. I didn't get the amount I wanted. So, I negotiated for more vacation days. I got 'em, and it made a huge difference in making me a loyal employee. I think SDRs should take at least one week per quarter off to recharge and rejuvenate.

Sales prospecting can be stressful. In the SDR role, reps get hung up on, lied to, and after a zillion discovery calls, told they are not getting the business. They also hear it from you when they don't perform. Extra vacation days can be the difference between staying the course or going insane.

Many SaaS companies offer unlimited personal time off (PTO). It can be a great recruiting tool as well as an important benefit to improve the mental health of your team.

Still, not every company offers unlimited PTO.

One company I worked for provided two weeks' vacation time on Day 1 of employment. That was a big selling point for candidates. Imagine starting a job and not having to wait six months to accrue enough time for a vacation.

Allowing more personal time off can be a great motivator for your SDR team. Americans could take a lesson from our European friends on this one. And there are several ways you can provide the time off including:

1. Allowing employees to negotiate more personal days off at annual reviews.
2. Creating sales contests that allow winners to win days off.
3. Providing vacation days to employees on Day 1 without the need to accrue time off.

What's great about providing extra vacation days is that it doesn't cost employers any additional cash. Most of the time, other employees cover for the vacationing SDR or the SDR puts in the necessary work before or after vacation to still hit quota.

Next up is another cost-free way to keep your team motivated.

Chapter 24

ATTIRE

Can the team's dress code really serve as a motivator? Without a doubt it can.

Does that mean every SDR should wear a suit? Or does it mean jeans and T-shirts should be the office attire? What about uniforms?

There are several owners and managers who believe the way you dress can make a big difference in how you act at work. There are many social and psychological studies about the subject as well. The truth is, it does matter but there is no one right way to dress.

I've worked in all kinds of environments. I worked in a Fortune 500 office that required a shirt and tie. A consulting firm I worked with had a business casual environment. I worked for another firm that allowed jeans every day, except for when clients were visiting. One firm allowed shorts on Fridays if employees donated two dollars to charity. I even worked from home in sweats (and sometimes just my boxers from the waist down). Gotta love those Zoom meetings.

If clients or prospects are not going to see you, you should be as comfortable as you can be without offending anyone. In business terms, that's casual attire. Jeans, T-shirts, and polo shirts are fine. Pajamas are not.

Allow me to be comfortable (on the phone or at home) and I will perform like nobody's business. Of course, business casual doesn't work for everyone.

For some SDRs, the way they dress influences how they behave. Require business suits and they are the most professional. Business casual might make them feel a little more relaxed, too relaxed to focus on hitting quota. And some who dress business casual might not get any work done at all.

There is no one right way to dress in a sales environment. Common sense tells us to dress professional when going out on sales calls or when there are visitors in the building.

When the team wears jeans, do they book more meetings? Guess what your office attire should be. If qualified opportunities are the highest when SDRs are dressed to the nines, the same applies. Whatever you choose, keep in mind that the way SDRs dress can be a motivator or demotivator, depending on who you ask.

Don't underestimate the power of an attire-themed day for your team. Sports jersey day. College sweatshirt day. Ugly sweater day. All are ways SDRs can have fun on the job while creating a team environment.

Being an open book is another way to motivate your team. More on that in the next chapter.

Chapter 25

TRANSPARENCY

I've worked for startups to small businesses to Fortune 500 companies. When working for either of these types of companies, being in the know of what's happening made a big difference. The smaller the company, the more transparent they were. One startup's CEO had a cubicle, that's right a cubicle, next to mine. They couldn't help but to be transparent.

Want to motivate your SDR team? Let them know the truth about what's going on in the business. Did you sign a new customer? Tell them about it. It'll motivate them to sell. Is the company creating a new management position? Let them know about it, even if they don't fit the criteria. Is the company earning its forecasted revenue? Or are layoffs coming soon? That could be discouraging news for them. However, you could also be in for a pleasant surprise.

For example, I worked for a company that knew the economy was in trouble. Instead of laying off a percentage of the staff, the president shared the company's dilemma. When he asked the company if they would be willing to take a five percent pay cut to help keep the company afloat, not a single person balked about it.

That company president's example is exactly the kind of transparency that can motivate an SDR to be loyal and to put in extra effort.

If you want to make the SDRs on your team feel more like a part of the team, be transparent about all the things you can.

There is a limit to what you can be transparent about. If executive leadership has given you information that is not to be shared, don't share it.

If sharing the information jeopardizes your job and your well-being, don't share it.

If the information can be perceived as negative and could result in mass resignations, don't share it.

Chapter 26

REFERRALS

To always hire A-Players sounds good in theory, but it's much more difficult to execute in real life. Why? A good amount of the A-Players are gainfully employed elsewhere. And some of the ones who are not A-Players do a pretty good job of posing as them during the interview process. Still, there are a couple of ways you can ensure that you continue to add A-Players to your sales team.

To start, managers should use psychometric testing, like Drive Test, for sales candidates. Psychometric testing included with reviewing resumes, interviewing, checking references, and even mock calls can increase your chances of hiring the right candidate.

In the book, "The Accidental Sales Manager," Chris Lytle shows data that states psychometric testing improves the chances of hiring the right salesperson by a huge percentage. When you think about it, everything else is simply relying on a gut feeling. When it comes to hiring stellar salespeople, how many times has your gut been wrong?

Another way to continue to hire A-Players is by continuously interviewing. One of my former bosses had a saying, "We're always interviewing and sometimes hiring." I love that statement because it's exactly the kind of mentality it takes to find diamonds, even if they're currently shining for another company.

Don't let the traditional nine-to-five hours keep you from finding the right candidate either. Managers and business owners must be willing to interview candidates during non-working hours too. For example, try hosting an after-hours open house. Or maybe you can meet a candidate at a restaurant near their home.

Remind SDRs of your internal referral program and how much money they can earn when they refer other SDRs. Chances are, your top SDRs know other top SDRs through previous employment, networking, or through professional organizations. If they help you find the perfect candidate, pay them what you would have paid a recruiter.

You might say, why do I want my current top performers to be threatened by new A-Players? It's a perfect way to help A-Players to maintain their level of excellence and to motivate the low performers to step up their game.

If you want to continue to hire A-Players so that the rest of your sales team stays motivated, follow these three suggestions, and watch your team grow with talent.

There is another no-cost way to reward SDRs. Turn to the next chapter to learn more.

Chapter 27

FREEDOM

Not every SDR must be managed. Yet there are managers who insist on "managing" every salesperson, even when they are always crushing their numbers.

Think of the entertainment industry. You've got people like Dwyane "The Rock" Johnson, Viola Davis, and Ryan Reynolds. They're the superstars who carry the movie. Oftentimes, they are the reason the fans pay money to see the movie, regardless of the plot. They get more freedom.

Then you have the lesser-known actors. Though they are good, their names alone won't bring in the crowd you need to make a profit or even break even. They get less freedom because they are more easily replaced.

In the SDR world, there are also superstars. Many of them have paid their dues and could outwork the rest of the team. And just like those movie stars, they might carry the team.

And they might work best when they are left alone to dominate. (These are the people you don't want to put your poor performers next to because it will totally throw your top people off their game.)

Some of them could even be great managers but choose to be individual performers.

Don't manage everyone the same way. Manage them based on their strengths, weaknesses, and learning style. Give top performers their freedom.

And just in case they want to share their knowledge with the team, the next chapter will explain how that can be a reward for them too.

Chapter 28

SOAPBOX

Sometimes managers only get a bird's eye view of a day in the life of an SDR. Yet some never ask the ones having success what they are doing. You'd be pleasantly surprised at the great ideas your staff have but don't share simply because you never asked. When SDRs feel valued, it gives them a great reason to stay motivated.

There are several ways your smart SDRs can share knowledge. One way is allowing them to conduct sales training meetings.

For example, when I was a top performer with one firm, I was often asked to conduct lunch and learn seminars for my colleagues. I would choose a topic that other salespeople were struggling with like overcoming objections, finding research sources, or using email to book more sales meetings. Sometimes the staff would bring their own lunch. Other times, management would pay for lunch.

The result was increased knowledge, full bellies, and a huge ego boost for me. Conducting training sessions made me feel special and valued. (Ehem, that's *Professor* Carpenter to you.)

But your SDR team doesn't have to give up an hour of their time to share their knowledge. During weekly meetings, you could choose a different SDR each time to share a trick or tip that they were able to use to help them become more effective.

Maybe someone could read from a book that they read or provide information from a conference or a webinar they participated in.

If it makes sense, ask your top performers who want to be leaders to serve as coaches.

Don't end your sales meetings by asking, "Does anyone have questions or comments?" The introverts who have good ideas will not speak up. Instead, go around the room and ask each person by name for comments or questions at the end of every meeting. Even if they don't have anything to say, the fact that you asked or even that you know their names might motivate them.

If members of your team have knowledge you believe is worth sharing, allow them to share it. It could be a huge ego boost for them.

The next chapter borrows a secret from some of the top SaaS organizations in the world on how to motivate SDRs and keep them happy.

Chapter 29

FOOD

Do you know why companies like Google and Apple give their employees free food? Sure, it saves their employees money and keeps them on the premises longer so that they can do more work. But food also changes employees' moods.

Have you ever noticed how you feel angrier when you're hungry? That's just your body's natural reaction. Now imagine your body's natural reaction to coffee in the morning, your favorite meal at lunch, or chocolate cake for dessert. I'll bet that it not only satisfies you but makes you happy.

Who is more productive, a happy employee or an unhappy employee? The answer is obvious. What's not so obvious is why more companies don't provide free food to employees.

There was a time in my life when I lived paycheck to paycheck as most Americans do. There was nothing worse than Thursdays before paydays because I knew my meals would suck as I was down to my last groceries. That got me thinking. What if the company provided free lunch to all employees the day before payday? Imagine how motivated they would be to come to work. Imagine how much more work these happy employees would do after a good meal. Combined with knowing they would get paid the following day would really make them happy.

Many startups have figured this out. They provide free meals at least once a week. One startup I worked for ordered lunch every Friday for our weekly meetings. Every Friday, we ate cuisine from different takeout restaurants. It was an amazing benefit, which added to the reasons why so many employees stayed loyal to the organization.

If you think buying food for the SDRs on your team is expensive, compare it to the cost of losing them. The Society for Human Resource Management (SHRM) says that it costs companies one and a half times an employee's salary or more when they leave. It makes sense when you think about the cost of training them, contributing to their benefits, hiring their replacements, and the cost of disrupting your customers' business. Surely a few pizzas every week would pale in comparison.

We've covered a lot of ways on how to motivate SDRs. In the next chapter, I will share some specific contests and SPIFFs that helped motivate my teams to achieve success.

Chapter 30

SPIFFS

The following is a list of SPIFF-based contests I've either run or read about online.

Make Quota Early - Pay a bonus for hitting quota in half the month. Pay less for hitting quota in three fourths of the month.

12 Days of SPIFFmas - Have a daily SPIFF for various KPIs hit for each of the 12 days before Christmas Eve.

Double Activities - Make double the calls and send double the emails to earn this reward.

Most Conversations - Encourage SDRs to get on the phone to talk to prospects. Reward the SPIFF for first-time convos regardless of the outcome.

Most Dials Before 10am - Help SDRs get an early start to their day by rewarding them.

Breakfast Club - Book two meetings before noon and the company will buy you breakfast up to $25.

BINGO - Select five common objections SDRs face over the phone. Reward them for attempting to overcome all five by sharing their recordings of conversations with prospects.

Triple Play- Reward SDRs for booking three meetings in three different ways, for example, phone call, email, and social media.

Beat the Boss- Hop on the phone and make some calls with your team. If they book more meetings than you for the day, reward them.

SDRs vs. AEs- Reward the team that books the most meetings within a certain amount of time.

People's Choice- Have the SDRs vote on which SDR has been the most helpful to them for a set period. Reward the top vote getter.

SDR of the Month - Reward for meetings, pipeline, and qualified opportunities but don't be afraid to change it up and reward SDRs for coaching, best improvement, referring new SDRs, or even for beating a PIP.

SDR of the Year - Go big on this reward. Make sure to include a plus one for any rewards involving travel, lodging, and dining.

First Adopter- Reward SDRs for being the first ones to try a new sales play or the first ones to use a new software.

Those are just a few of the SPIFFs I've used or heard about that got SDRs excited to come to work. Just remember,

SPIFFs are typically rewards for short-term behavior. If there is a behavior you're looking to change within your SDR team, a SPIFF contest just may do the trick.

To encourage longer-term behavioral changes, you'll need to adjust your comp plan and more. Otherwise, collaborate with your HR team to see about adding some benefits that get SDRs excited about coming to work every day.

Part 4

CAREER

Chapter 31

NEXT?

There will come a time in your SDR Manager career when you will ask yourself, 'What's next?'

Maybe you crushed it in the manager role. You exceeded your pipeline goals. SDRs on your team sourced the most Closed Won deals at the company. You prepared several SDRs for the AE role, and they were promoted. You even mentored some SDRs into managers themselves.

HOW TO MEASURE YOUR SUCCESS

As an SDR Manager, your success will be determined by the success of your team. That can be measured in several ways. Let's look at the most common measurements of success below.

PIPELINE ATTAINMENT VERSUS GOAL

Pipeline attainment versus goal is a fairly simple way to measure the success of your team. Your boss should give you this goal before the start of each quarter. The pipeline goal can come from an agreement from Sales, Marketing, and Finance.

For example, your team's quarterly pipeline goal could be $2 million. If the team only brings in $1.5 million in pipeline, you'll be at 75% of goal. If they bring in $3 million in pipeline, you'll be at 150% of goal. The latter is great if you have accelerators or uncapped commission in your comp plan.

Many SaaS organizations have moved to this measurement of success for SDR Managers. The problem with it though is that SDRs don't determine pipeline dollars. Pipeline is determined by AEs. There's nothing wrong with that if they enter the true value of the deal. Some AEs enter a lesser amount if they are held accountable for closing a specific percentage of pipeline. I've even seen AEs create opportunities with zero-dollar values.

If you are measured and paid based on pipeline, it means that you have less control over your own destiny. Therefore, some SDR Managers push back on being measured and compensated based on pipeline.

QUALIFIED OPPS ATTAINMENT VERSUS GOAL

Another way to measure your success is by determining the number of qualified opportunities your team helped create versus the team's goal.

For example, let's say you have ten SDRs on your team and each of them have a quota of five qualified opps per month. Your monthly goal comes out to 50 qualified opps. Your quarterly goal would be 150 qualified opps. Hit 120 opportunities for the quarter, and you'll be sitting at 80% of quota. Get 200 and you'll be at 133% of quota.

If you have a solid SLA in place with your AEs that determines what a qualified opportunity is and when AEs need to convert meetings to opps, you'll find that this is a good way to measure success.

If there is no such SLA in place, you'll have less control over your own destiny once again.

FIRST-TIME COMPLETED MEETINGS ATTAINMENT VERSUS GOAL

To get to qualified opportunities, your team must first set up meetings with prospects and AEs. This is the reason SDR teams exist.

We're talking about meetings that prospects showed up for not meetings that were scheduled but didn't happen.

For example, if your team of ten SDRs have a quota of ten completed meetings per month, your goal is 100 meetings per month. Your quarterly goal would be 300 meetings.

If your team ends up with 250 meetings in the quarter, you'll be sitting at 83% of quota. If they get 350 meetings, you'll be at 116% of quota.

I like this measurement of success the most because it is totally in your team's control. You don't have to wait for AEs to create an opportunity. You don't have to wait for AEs to assign a dollar value to the opportunity.

PERCENTAGE OF SDRS HITTING OR EXCEEDING QUOTA

Though SDR Managers aren't normally comped by this metric, many executive leaders look at the percentage of SDRs on your team that are hitting or exceeding quota. It could be based on pipeline, qualified opportunities, or meetings.

This metric helps to determine your coaching effectiveness. This is the reason a solid coaching framework is a must.

For me, if 70% of your team is hitting or exceeding quota, you're doing a good job. Other leaders might want a greater percentage of your team hitting quota to determine success.

Again, it's not so great for determining commission but it's a good metric to use in monthly and quarterly reviews.

A BLENDED APPROACH

One company I worked for used a blended approach. The SDR Manager at an emergency alerting software company was measured by pipeline attainment and completed meetings. It was a 50/50 split.

For example, if their monthly OTE was $3000, they would earn $1500 for hitting 100% of their pipeline goals and another $1500 for hitting their meetings goals.

Many SaaS organizations use blended goals for SDR Manager compensation plans.

WHAT IF YOU'RE NOT CRUSHING IT

PIPs for SDR Managers

If your manager feels that you are underperforming, you could be put on a PIP. PIPs are determined by underperformance or by not hitting your goals.

Some leaders automatically put SDR Managers on a PIP if any SDR on their team goes on one. It helps hold managers accountable for SDRs' individual success. I'm not a fan of this strategy. I think success or failure should be determined by the entire team's performance.

But if I was put on a PIP because of one SDR's performance, best believe I would be coaching them like Phil Jackson coached Kobe Bryant and Michael Jordan. I'd be trying to find them all the warm leads I could. I might even do some outbounding on their accounts.

I prefer to use a grading system like the schools. I think performing under 70% should be the metric used. If an SDR Manager's team hits under 70% of goal for the quarter, they should go on a PIP.

Some leaders like to look at the last four month's performance or the last six month's performance instead. If the average of either falls below 70%, the manager is put on a PIP.

I'm sure this won't apply to you. You wouldn't be reading this book if you accepted underachievement. But it's nice to know how leaders think about the good and the bad of SDR Managers' performance and how it is measured.

Perhaps management wasn't all it was cracked up to be.

Or maybe you simply burned out.

What's next will depend on you. It will depend on your success in the role. It will depend on your career aspirations. And it will depend on your mental state after a specific amount of time.

Get Better at Leading

The SDR Manager role may be your first leadership position. Though some people can handle managing, only a few are capable of leading.

Remember when I said I started a neighborhood electric football league, started a band, captained a tennis team, and led a military squad? They were great real-world leadership experiences. It didn't mean I was ready to go and lead a sales development team.

I needed more training.

I took courses at Sales Academy on how to be an effective leader.

One employer put me through a course on authentic leadership.

Another put me through Sandler leadership training.

I read books like *Radical Candor, Influencer,* and *The First 90 Days* all on my own because I wanted to be a great leader.

I took advantage of my company's free access to LinkedIn Learning. Took a few courses on leadership and earned certifications.

I attended webinars led by respected leaders like the Chief Revenue Officer at Gong and the founder of the American Association of Inside Sales Professionals (AA-ISP).

I've taken a gazillion psychometric tests like DISC to find out what type of leader I am and how I should best get along with others.

And I continue to learn.

If what's next for you is to become a great SDR Manager, you've got to become a fan of continuous education.

Keep learning.

Keep stretching.

Keep strengthening your brain.

Take a course on change management because the changes will keep coming. You'll need to manage your team's expectations.

What if you've decided you don't want to be an SDR Manager anymore? (I told you the changes would keep coming.)

There are three roles I highly recommend you pursue after being an SDR Manager.

Account Executive

There are three reasons I suggest SDR Managers become AEs after their stint in leadership.

The first reason is that you might need a break from leadership. Remember how good it was to only be accountable for yourself? Nobody was asking for your help over Slack every 20 minutes. There wasn't any PTO to approve. No PIPs to write. No explaining to executive leadership why the team's numbers are down.

SDR leadership may have helped you realize what you don't want to do long term: leading people.

And that's okay.

The second reason you want to consider becoming an AE is because it will help round out your sales career.

If you were promoted from the SDR role to SDR Manager position without getting a chance to close deals, you are probably less likely to empathize with AEs. You also missed the rush of being one of the reasons the company brought in revenue. If SDRs are considered a bench for the AE role at your company, you are training them for a role in which you have no experience.

The third reason you want experience as an AE is that you may need to lead AEs in the next chapter of your career. You will stand a better chance of leading AEs directly or with leading teams that include AEs if you've been one yourself.

Full disclosure here: During my 13-year stint as an SDR, I spent a few months here and there as an AE. One time it was voluntary because I was simply burned out as an SDR, so I asked for the change.

The other time it was forced upon me as the closers were struggling, and we needed more revenue. The VP of Sales thought we could generate more revenue if SDRs became true inside sales reps responsible for closing small deals.

Before I started working for tech firms, I sold orthopedic shoes. It was a blend of account management and new business development.

I did okay as a closer but to be honest, it wasn't for me. The pressure to bring in revenue was too much. The long sales cycles made it feel like it took forever to earn a commission check. Plus, I never had the advantage of having an SDR book qualified meetings for me. But if I was called upon to lead a team that had AEs, I would feel much more prepared because of that experience.

Sales Enablement Manager

I like to think of sales enablement managers as the internal sales teachers. They onboard and train AEs and SDRs. They prepare curriculums and lesson plans. They teach people how to use the software in your stack.

As a coach, trainer, and administrator, you're already doing a lot of the duties of a sales enablement manager. If you work for a start-up without a sales enablement team, you're doing even more of those duties.

That's why the transition is natural for SDR Managers.

Sales enablement managers can go on to be directors or VPs of either sales enablement or sales operations.

Manager of Managers

When successful SDRs become SDR Managers, they are able to share all the things that made them successful based on firsthand experience. The same thing happens when SDR Managers get promoted to Director of Business Development or VP of Sales Development.

Sharing what made you successful as a manager can make you an awesome Director or VP. However, that's just a taste of the role.

You'll also need to be able to put a successful coaching framework in place, coach your coaches, be accountable for each of your managers' team pipeline, and become an expert in forecasting and presenting data to executive leadership.

If your team includes AEs, you'll have to know how to coach AEs through deal progression, work with Legal and Finance to help deals move along and be accountable for the overall revenue of your team.

You still need to be a great people manager and a great diplomat across teams. In fact, you will find yourself doing some of the same duties as an SDR Manager just on a grander scale.

At this level, nobody will expect you to do any outbounding. But if you do, you will earn beau coup respect from the SDRs your managers lead.

Although the position can be stressful at times, it can also be financially rewarding. When I became a director, I doubled the income of my first SDR Manager job.

Other Paths

There are other non-traditional paths you might decide to take after the SDR Manager job.

You might decide that you missed the SDR role and return to it.

You may join the Marketing team and become a Demand Generation Manager or a Social Media Manager. Writing cadences, emails, and social media posts are a good start.

You might even decide to strike out on your own and start your own business.

Or, hey, you may just stay put at your first-line manager job because your calling is to lead and coach others. That's fine too.

This is why you should never stop learning.

While getting a four-year degree, Master's degree, or even a doctorate level degree could be rewarding, a traditional education is not always required for continuous learning.

Start with webinars, in-person events, and online courses. You can find free or inexpensive courses through resources like edX, Coursera, Udemy, LinkedIn Learning, Pluralsight, and HubSpot Academy. You can learn without the time commitment a traditional education may require.

Check out documentaries that feature great leaders and great coaches like *Belichick & Saban: The Art of Coaching.*

And don't forget about books.

If you are considering a career change, you may want to start obtaining certifications in the field you are looking to join. There are several courses to choose from.

Whatever you decide to do, I'm sure you will be great at it.

Thank you for taking the time to invest in the purchasing and reading of this book. Be sure to find me on social media and connect. I'd love to hear your story. Thank you for letting me share mine.

Made in the USA
Las Vegas, NV
07 April 2024

88376961R00129